Science

The 13+ Practice Book

For the Common Entrance 13+ exams

How to get your free Online Practice Papers

Just go to **cgpbooks.co.uk/extras** and enter this code...

1769 6235 3209 4345

By the way, this code only works for one person. If somebody else has used this book before you, they might have already claimed the Practice Papers.

CGP

Practise • Prepare • Pass

Everything your child needs for 13+ success

CONTENTS

✓ Use the tick boxes to check off the topics you've completed.

Published by CGP

Editors:
Sarah Armstrong, Mary Falkner, Emily Garrett, Rachel Kordan,
Sarah Pattison, Ethan Starmer-Jones, Charlotte Whiteley

Contributor:
James Wallis

With thanks to Janet Cruse-Sawyer, Glenn Rogers and Karen Wells for the proofreading.
With thanks to Ana Pungartnik for the copyright research.

ISBN: 978 1 78294 824 7

Printed by Elanders Ltd, Newcastle upon Tyne.
Clipart from Corel®

From original material by Paddy Gannon.

How to Use This Book

Have a look at the following information — it might just come in handy...

There are **Two Levels** in **Common Entrance 13+ Science**

1) You can either do **Level 1** or **Level 2** exams for **Common Entrance 13+ Science**. The Level 2 exams are a bit **harder**.

2) You'll do **one paper** for the **Level 1** exam, and it tests you on all three science subjects (Biology, Chemistry and Physics).

3) You'll do **three separate papers** for the **Level 2** exam — one for each of the three sciences.

You Might Sit the **CASE Paper**

1) You **could** be entered for the **Common Academic Scholarship Exam** (CASE).

2) You'll do **one paper** for CASE. It has **three sections** — one for each of **Biology**, **Chemistry** and **Physics**.

No matter which exam you do, at least 25% of each paper tests your knowledge of Working Scientifically.

This Book Has Some **Useful Features**

This book is split up into **13 sections**. Each section is split into different **topics**, so you can practise the bits you need.

For calculation questions, there's space to do your **working**.

Use this space to write your **answer**. The number tells you how many **marks** this question or question part is worth.

Use the **detailed answers** (p.116) to mark your work. Write your **score** in the box at the end of each topic.

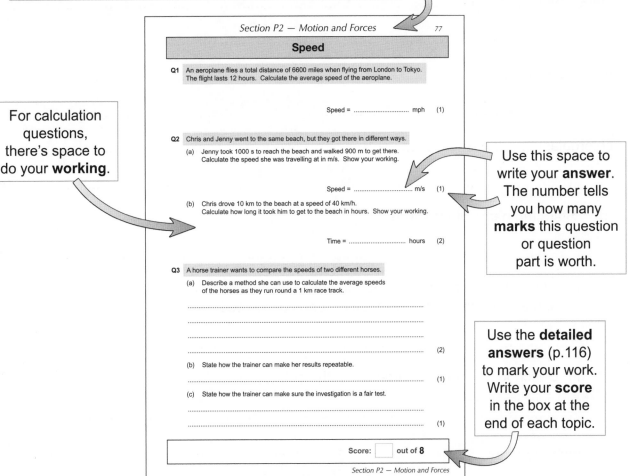

There's also a full set of **practice papers** available online. You'll find a code to access these at the start of this book.

How to Use This Book

Cells

Q1   The diagram below shows a typical plant cell.

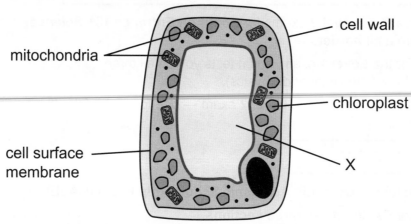

(a)   State the functions of the following parts of the cell.

cell wall: ....

....

cell surface membrane: ....

....

mitochondria: ....

....

chloroplast: ....

....   **(4)**

(b)   State the name of structure X.

....   **(1)**

(c) (i)   Name the component of both an animal cell
            and a plant cell that contains the genes of the cell.

....   **(1)**

(ii)   Describe the function of genes in the cell.

....

....   **(1)**

Score: ☐ **out of 7**

More on Cells and Diffusion

Q1 The diagram below shows the levels of organisation in a plant.

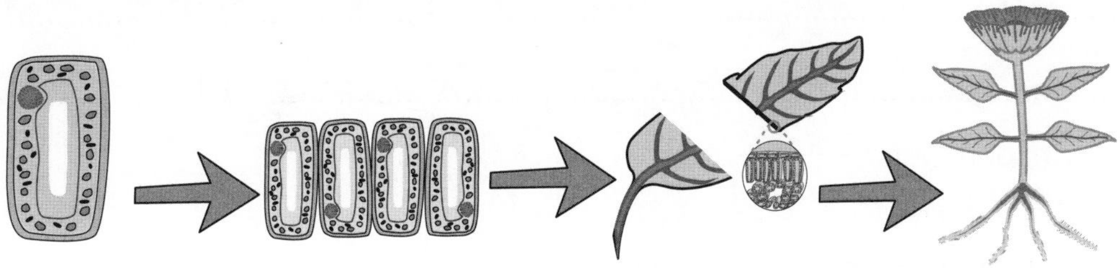

....

organ	**tissue**	**organism**	**cell**

(a) Use the words from the box above to label the diagram. (1)

(b) The root system is an example of an organ system in plants.
Describe what an organ system is.

....

.... (1)

Q2 Below is a diagram of a Euglena.
Euglena are unicellular organisms that live in water.

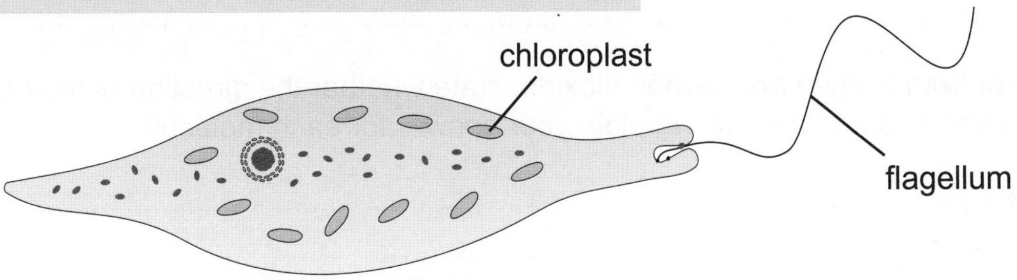

(a) Describe what unicellular means.

.... (1)

(b) Euglena have several adaptations that help them to survive in their environment.
Explain how the following adaptations help Euglena to survive.

(i) the flagellum

....

.... (1)

(ii) the chloroplasts

....

.... (1)

(c) Amoeba are another unicellular organism.
Describe how they are adapted to feed.

....

....

.... (1)

Q3 The diagram below shows an animal cell.
The cell contains molecules of oxygen and carbon dioxide.

○ = carbon dioxide
● = oxygen

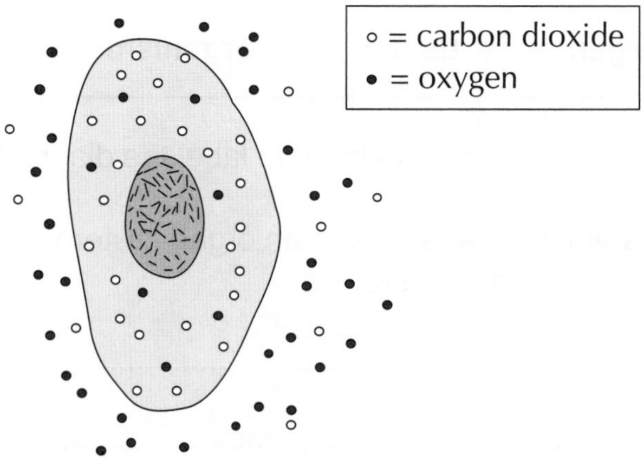

(a) Name the part of the cell that the gas molecules
have to pass through to enter or leave the cell.

.... (1)

(b) For both oxygen and carbon dioxide, state whether the direction of movement
is into or out of the cell. Explain your answer for each molecule.

Oxygen: ....

....

....

Carbon dioxide: ....

....

.... (4)

(c) Describe the movement of glucose molecules when the cell respires.

.... (1)

Score: [   ] out of **12**

Section B1 — Structure and Function of Living Organisms

The Light Microscope

Q1 Anita is preparing a microscope slide of some onion cells using water.

(a) Describe the steps Anita should take to prepare the slide.

....

....

....

....

.... (3)

eyepiece lens

rough focusing knob

objective lens

stage

fine focusing knob

mirror

(b) Anita places the slide on the stage of a microscope.
She angles the mirror so that light shines up through the hole.
Give one safety precaution she should take when changing the mirror angle.

....

.... (1)

(c) Describe how Anita could focus the microscope on the onion cells.

....

....

....

.... (3)

(d) The nuclei of onion cells are quite difficult to see.
Name a stain that Anita could add to the slide to see the nuclei more clearly.

.... (1)

Score: ☐ out of **8**

Nutrition

Q1 A balanced human diet contains many different nutrients. Underline the function of each of the following nutrients.

(a) Carbohydrates are needed for

preventing constipation **insulation**

growth and repair of tissues **energy**

(1)

(b) Proteins are needed for

preventing constipation **insulation**

growth and repair of tissues **energy**

(1)

(c) Lipids are needed for

preventing constipation **repair of tissues**

growth **energy and insulation**

(1)

Q2 There are seven important components of a healthy human diet.

(a) Complete the table below to show which component of a healthy diet each food is a good source of. Use each component once.

Food Source	Component
Oranges	Vitamins
Butter	
Fish	
Coffee	
Potatoes	
Table salt	
Carrots	

(6)

(b) State the name of a test you could use to see if starch is present in a food sample.

.... (1)

Score: ☐ out of **10**

Section B1 — Structure and Function of Living Organisms

Staying Healthy

Q1 An unbalanced diet can lead to deficiency diseases.

(a) (i) Underline the word which correctly completes the following sentence.

Calcium salts are an example of a

lipid   **protein**   **vitamin**   **mineral**   (1)

(ii) Describe the effect a lack of calcium can have on human health.

....

.... (1)

(b) State the deficiency disease caused by a lack of vitamin C.

.... (1)

Q2 Health problems can be caused by eating too much or too little food.

(a) Explain what can happen if a person doesn't eat enough food.

....

....

.... (2)

(b) Eating too much food can cause obesity.
(i) State two health problems that obesity can lead to.

1. ....

2. .... (2)

(ii) Describe the potential effect on the body of eating too much saturated fat.

....

.... (1)

(c) Foods high in sugar can provide too much energy.
Name the solution that can be used to test if a food contains sugar.

.... (1)

Score: [   ] out of **9**

Gas Exchange

Q1 Below is a diagram of the human gas exchange system.

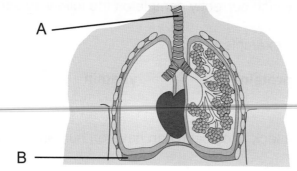

(a) Name the tube (A) that brings air into and out of the body.

.... (1)

(b) Name the muscle B.

.... (1)

(c) (i) Explain what happens when muscle B contracts.

....

....

.... (2)

(ii) Name the stage of the breathing process that this represents.

.... (1)

(d) Describe what happens during expiration.

....

....

.... (2)

(e) The inner surface of the lungs is folded to give the lungs a large surface area for gas exchange.
(i) State the name of the small air sacs made by these folds.

.... (1)

(ii) Give two other ways that the lungs are well adapted for gas exchange.

1. ....

2. .... (2)

Q2 Smoking can damage the lungs.

(a) Give two diseases which are caused by smoking.

1. ....

2. .... (2)

(b) Smoking damages the surface of the lungs.
Suggest the effect this can have on a person's breathing. Explain your answer.

....

....

.... (2)

Q3 Laura wants to see how exercise affects her heart rate. To carry out her investigation, she connects herself to a monitor that continually records her heart rate. She sits still for five minutes before using an exercise bike for one minute. After the one minute she sits still again. Part of the results given by the monitor are shown in the graph below.

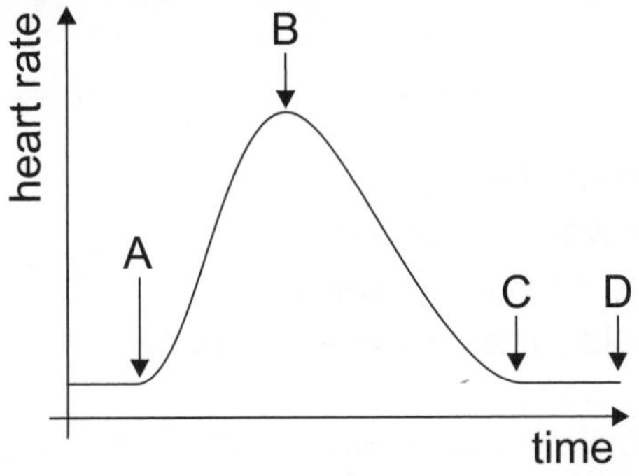

(a) State which label on the graph shows the point at which Laura started using the exercise bike. Explain your answer.

Label: ....

Explanation: .... (2)

(b) (i) Describe how Laura's breathing rate would have changed during the time on the exercise bike.

.... (1)

(ii) Explain why this change occurs.

....

....

.... (2)

(c) Describe the effect of exercising regularly on lung volume.

.... (1)

Section B1 — Structure and Function of Living Organisms

Q4 Jackson wants to know how much air he breathes out in a normal breath.
He measures the volume of his exhaled breath five times using a measuring cylinder, a tank of water and a plastic tube. His results are shown in the table below.

Repeat	1	2	3	4	5
Volume (cm³)	450	525	470	485	415

(a) Calculate the mean volume of one of Jackson's exhaled breaths when breathing normally.

Mean volume = ... cm³   (1)

(b) Explain why it is important that Jackson takes several repeat measurements.

....

....   (2)

(c) State whether Jackson's results are precise. Explain your answer.

....

....   (1)

(d) A spirometer is shown on the right.
Jackson's friend Kate wants to use a spirometer to measure her vital capacity.
Describe how she could measure vital capacity.

....   (1)

(e) Kate has asthma. Describe what may happen to her airways if she breathes in a substance that her airways are sensitive to.

....

....

....

....   (3)

(f) Kate carries an inhaler with her in case she has an asthma attack.
Explain how her inhaler helps during an asthma attack.

....

....   (1)

Score: ☐ out of **29**

Section B1 — Structure and Function of Living Organisms

Growing Up

Q1 Underline the structure that correctly completes the following sentence.

In females, egg cells are released from the

ovaries   **fallopian tube**   **vagina**   **uterus**   (1)

Q2 The diagram shows the male reproductive system.

(a) Label the following structures on the diagram.

| sperm duct |
| urethra |

(2)

Testis

(b) State what a gamete is.

.... (1)

(c) Give the name of the male gametes.

.... (1)

(d) Describe the function of the testes.

.... (1)

Q3 Girls and boys both go through puberty between the ages of 10 and 16.

(a) Describe three changes that occur to girls during puberty.

1. ....

2. ....

3. .... (3)

(b) Describe three changes that occur to boys during puberty.

1. ....

2. ....

3. .... (3)

(c) Explain why the physical changes of puberty occur.

.... (1)

Score: [   ] out of **13**

The Menstrual Cycle

Q1 The diagram below shows the main stages of the menstrual cycle.

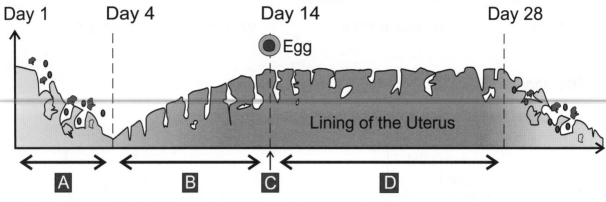

Day 1   Day 4   Day 14   Day 28

Egg

Lining of the Uterus

A   B   C   D

(a)   Underline the letter that corresponds to each of the following stages of the menstrual cycle.

   (i)   The lining of the uterus builds up.

      A   **B**   **C**   **D**   (1)

   (ii) The thick lining of the uterus breaks down and blood flows out (menstruation).

      A   **B**   **C**   **D**   (1)

   (iii) The egg is travelling down the oviduct to be fertilised.

      A   **B**   **C**   **D**   (1)

   (iv) The lining of the uterus is very thick and full of blood.

      A   **B**   **C**   **D**   (1)

(b)   Explain why the lining of the uterus needs to become thick.

....

.... (1)

(c)   Use the diagram to work out how long it takes the uterus lining to build up again after menstruation.

.... (1)

(d)   State on which day of the menstrual cycle the egg is released.

.... (1)

Score: [   ] out of **7**

Having a Baby

Q1 Underline the structure that correctly completes the following sentence.

Sperm cells meet egg cells in the

ovaries   **fallopian tube**   **vagina**   **uterus**   (1)

Q2 To have a baby, sperm need to be released inside the female.

(a) Describe how sexual intercourse brings sperm and eggs together.

....

....

....   (2)

(b) Compare the numbers of sperm and eggs released.

....

....   (1)

(c) Describe what happens when an egg is fertilised.

....

....

....   (2)

(d) State the name given to a fertilised egg.

....   (1)

(e) Describe how an egg becomes an embryo.

....

....   (1)

Q3 Freya and Hussain have three children.
None of their children are identical to either of them.

Explain the reason for this.

....

....   (1)

Q4 The diagram below shows a fetus attached to its mother.

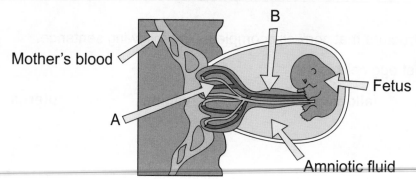

(a) (i) State the name of the structure marked A on the diagram.

.... (1)

(ii) State the name of the structure marked B on the diagram.

.... (1)

(b) Underline the option to complete the sentence below.

The 9 months in which the fetus develops in the uterus is known as **gestation**
fertilisation .

(1)

(c) Describe the function of the amniotic fluid.

....

.... (1)

(d) Explain the importance of the placenta.

....

....

....

.... (3)

(e) Explain why expectant mothers are advised not to smoke or drink alcohol
during their pregnancy.

....

....

.... (2)

Score: [ ] out of **18**

Section B1 — Structure and Function of Living Organisms

Plant Reproduction and Seeds

Q1 The picture below shows a flower. Some parts of the flower are labelled with letters.

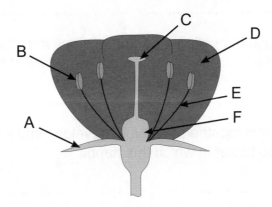

(a) (i) State which letter points to the sepal.

.... (1)

(ii) State which letter points to the part that contains ovules.

.... (1)

(iii) Name the male part of the flower.

.... (1)

(iv) Name the part labelled B.

.... (1)

(b) The plant is pollinated by insects. Describe how insects pollinate the flower.

....

....

.... (3)

(c) Name another method that flowers can be pollinated by.
Explain two adaptations a flower may have to be pollinated in this way.

Method: ....

Adaptation 1: ....

....

Adapatation 2: ....

.... (3)

Q2 Plants need to be pollinated to produce seeds.

(a) Describe the meaning of the term pollination.

....

.... (1)

(b) After passing through the pollen tube, the nucleus from the male sex cell fuses with the nucleus of a female egg cell. State the name of this process.

.... (1)

(c) After the sex cells join together, the ovule develops into a seed.
State the part of the flower in which this happens.

.... (1)

(d) Each seed contains a food store. Name two other parts of a seed.

1. ....

2. .... (2)

(e) The seed starts to grow into a small plant. State the name of this process.

.... (1)

Q3 Plants have developed various methods to carry their seeds far from the parent plant. The pictures below show fruits from a tomato plant and a dandelion plant.

bright red skin

parachute

Tomato   Dandelion

For each fruit, use the information in the picture to suggest whether each fruit is animal-dispersed or wind-dispersed. Explain your answers.

Tomato: ....

....

Dandelion: ....

.... (2)

Section B1 — Structure and Function of Living Organisms

Q4 Some students investigated whether the size of sycamore fruit affects the distance to which the seeds are dispersed. They made paper models of the fruits with different lengths of wings and dropped them from a height of 1 metre. There was a fan at a set distance behind the person dropping the models.

(a) State the type of seed dispersal the students are investigating.

.... (1)

(b) (i) Name the dependent variable in this experiment.

.... (1)

(ii) Name the independent variable in this experiment.

.... (1)

(c) The results of the experiment are shown in the graph below.

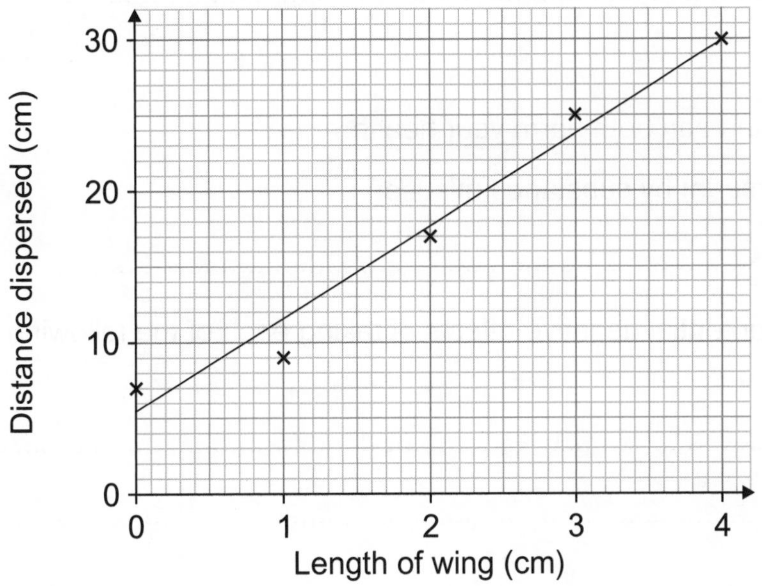

(i) How much further did the model with the longest wings travel than the one with no wings?

.... (1)

(ii) What can you conclude about the size of sycamore fruit and dispersal?

....

.... (1)

(d) Suggest how the students could make their results more reliable.

.... (1)

Score: ☐ out of **24**

Healthy Living

Q1 Underline the statement below that is false.

All recreational drugs are illegal.   **Drugs affect behaviour.**

Drugs can damage your health.   **Caffeine is a drug.**   (1)

Q2 Tobacco contains a recreational drug.

(a)   State what is meant by a recreational drug.

....   (1)

(b)   Name the recreational drug contained in tobacco.

....   (1)

Q3 Alcohol and marijuana can both harm your health.

(a)   State what is meant by substance misuse.

....   (1)

(b)   Describe two potential negative effects of taking each of the following drugs:
(i) Alcohol

1. ....

2. ....   (2)

(ii) Marijuana

1. ....

2. ....   (2)

Q4 Explain how exercise helps to prevent obesity.

....

....

....   (2)

| Score: | | out of **10** |

Fighting Disease

Q1 Viruses and bacteria can cause disease.

(a) (i) Give an example of a viral disease.

.... (1)

(ii) Give an example of a bacterial disease.

.... (1)

(b) Describe how viruses can affect health.

....

....

.... (2)

(c) Describe how bacteria can affect health.

....

....

.... (2)

Q2 Disease has a negative impact on human health and wellbeing.
Prevention is often the most effective way of stopping the spread of disease.

(a) A mumps virus enters the body of someone who has had the mumps vaccination.
Explain why the person would be unlikely to become ill with mumps.

....

.... (1)

(b) Disease can also be prevented by other methods
such as washing hands and having laws targeting
places where food is made. Describe how
these methods act as a defence against disease.

....

....

....

.... (3)

Score: _____ out of **10**

Plant Nutrition

Q1   Photosynthesis is a process that allows plants to produce food.

(a)   For each part below, underline the option that completes the sentence.
(i)   One of the reactants in photosynthesis is

hydrogen   **water**   **glucose**   **oxygen**   (1)

(ii)   The green chemical that allows plants to absorb light energy is called

carbon dioxide   **glucose**   **chlorophyll**   **nitrogen**   (1)

(b)   Write the word equation that summarises what happens in photosynthesis.

....   (1)

(c)   Most plants convert the sugar produced in photosynthesis to a different chemical to make it easier to store. State the name of this chemical.

....   (1)

Q2   Plants contain specialised cells and structures that are essential for their survival.

(a)   Holes in the surface of leaves allow gases to pass in and out of them. State the name of these holes.

....   (1)

(b)   One component of a plant cell contains chlorophyll. State the name of this component and describe its function.

....   (2)

(c)   Describe the role of the xylem in a plant.

....   (1)

(d)   State the name of the structures in plants that transport sugars.

....   (1)

(e)   Plants absorb water and minerals through their roots.
(i)   Name a feature of root hair cells that increases their rate of absorption.

....   (1)

(ii)   Name two minerals absorbed through the roots and state what they are used for.

....
....   (2)

Q3 Jill wants to see whether a chilli plant grows faster when watered once a week or twice a week. She decides to buy two chilli plants for her investigation. She finds the plants below at her local market.

(a) State which two chilli plants she should use for her experiment. Explain your answer.

Plants: ....

Reason: ....

.... (2)

(b) Describe a method Jill could use for her investigation.

....

.... (2)

Q4 Anand is planning to carry out an investigation on photosynthesis. Anand says "as the intensity of light shining on a plant increases, the amount of light energy absorbed by the plant and used for photosynthesis also increases".

Anand carries out an experiment to measure the amount of oxygen produced by a plant over a period of 12 hours. He then uses his data to calculate the plant's average rate of photosynthesis. He repeats his experiment for different intensities of light whilst keeping all other variables constant. His results are shown in the graph on the right.

(a) Underline the option that completes the sentence below.

The statement given by Anand is his **hypothesis** / **prediction** . (1)

(b) State one way in which the data collected in the graph supports Anand's statement, and one way in which it does not.

Supports: ....

Does not support: .... (2)

Score: ☐ out of **19**

Photosynthesis Experiments

Q1 The diagram on the right shows an experiment to study photosynthesis in pond weed. Bubbles made by the plant were collected in the measuring cylinder.

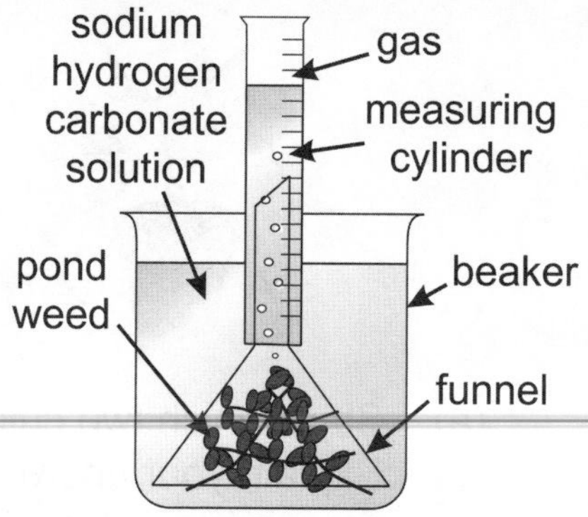

(a) Name the gas collected in the measuring cylinder.

.... (1)

(b) Describe how this gas is tested for.

....

.... (1)

(c) A student decides to use the technique demonstrated in the diagram above to compare the amount of gas produced by a number of different water plants. State two precautions the student should take to ensure this is a fair test.

1. ....

2. .... (2)

Q2 Tom decides to carry out an experiment to show that light is needed for starch production in plants. He places a leafy plant in a closed cupboard for 24 hours. He then places black tape on one of the leaves and puts the plant on a well-lit windowsill. He leaves it there for another 24 hours, then removes the leaf from the plant and peels off the black tape.

(a) Explain why Tom leaves the plant in a cupboard for a day.

.... (1)

(b) State what colour iodine changes to when exposed to starch.

.... (1)

(c) Describe how Tom can use iodine to show that there's no starch on the part of the leaf that was covered with tape.

....

....

....

....

.... (4)

Score: ▢ out of **10**

The Importance of Plants

Q1 Underline the organism below that is able to photosynthesise.

algae   **grasshopper**   **glow worm**   **snake**   (1)

Q2 Some chickens are fed on grain from a crop grown in a nearby field. Explain how the crop uses the Sun's energy to become a source of energy for the chickens.

....

....

....   (3)

Q3 In the 18th century, Joseph Priestley conducted an important experiment in which he placed two mice in sealed bell jars. He also placed a plant in one of the jars.

After a while, mouse A collapsed, while mouse B did not.

(a)   Explain the results of this experiment.

....

....

....

....   (3)

(b)   Explain how this experiment demonstrates the global importance of plants for life on Earth.

....

....

....   (1)

Score: [   ] out of **8**

Carbon Cycle

Q1 Carbon is recycled in a process called the carbon cycle.

(a) Underline the answer that completes the sentence below.

Carbon dioxide is removed from the atmosphere when...

...plants photosynthesise.

...plants respire.

...animals respire.

...fuel is burnt. (1)

(b) Describe how carbon is passed on from plants to animals.

.... (1)

(c) Explain how carbon is passed on to animals which do not eat plants.

.... (1)

(d) Part of the carbon cycle is shown below.

Plant and animal remains are left. ⟶ **X** ⟶ Combustion by humans.

Describe the process represented by **X**.

....

.... (1)

(e) Describe the role of decomposers in the carbon cycle.

....

.... (2)

(f) Explain what happens to the level of carbon dioxide in the atmosphere if too many fossil fuels are burnt.

....

.... (2)

Score: [ ] out of **8**

Aerobic Respiration

Q1 Breathing and respiration are both essential for animal survival.

(a) Describe the two processes of breathing and respiration.

....

.... (2)

(b) The diagram below shows a typical animal cell in which respiration takes place.

cytoplasm   nucleus

cell surface
membrane   mitochondria

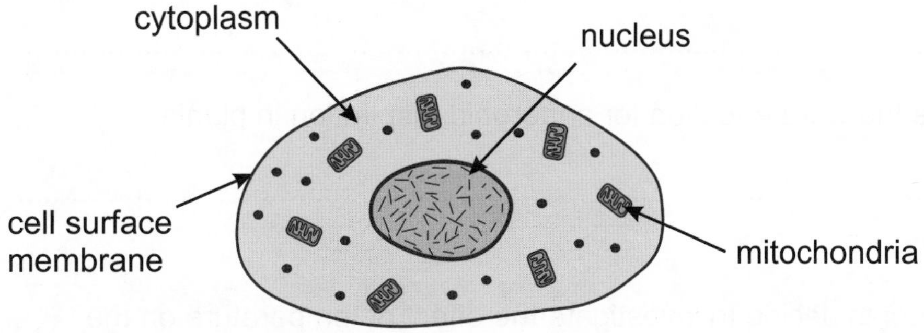

State the word equation for aerobic respiration.

.... (1)

(c) State where in the cell aerobic respiration takes place.

.... (1)

(d) Describe how the reactants for aerobic respiration are obtained
by the body and transported to sites of respiration.

....

.... (2)

(e) Describe a simple experiment to show that the main gas produced
in aerobic respiration is present in exhaled air.

....

....

.... (2)

(f) Give one use of energy in the body.

.... (1)

Score: ☐ out of **9**

Anaerobic Respiration

Q1 Organisms can respire aerobically and anaerobically.

(a) Describe the differences between aerobic respiration
and anaerobic respiration in humans.

....

....

....

.... (4)

(b) Write the word equation for anaerobic respiration in plants.

.... (1)

Q2 Some students decide to investigate the effect of temperature on the
rate of fermentation in yeast. They set up the experiment shown below.

They counted the number of bubbles produced in boiling tube B in one minute.
They then repeated the procedure at different temperatures by changing the
temperature of the water bath.

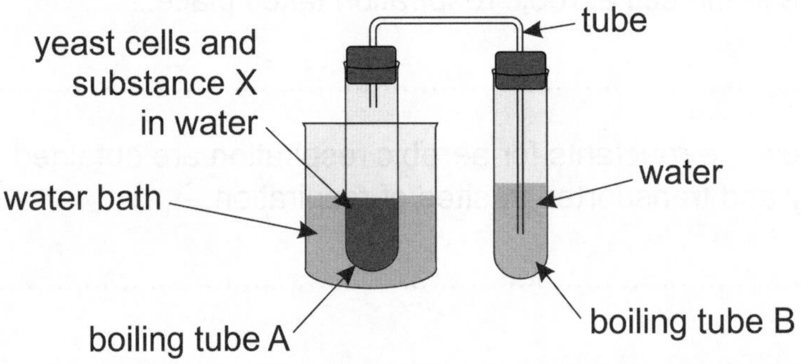

(a) Suggest what substance X could be and explain your answer.

.... (1)

(b) State the dependent variable in this experiment.

.... (1)

(c) Suggest how the students could make their results more accurate.

....

.... (1)

Score: [   ] out of **8**

Interdependence and Food Webs

Q1   Complete the sentences below by underlining the best option.

(a)   Organisms that can make their own food are called

carnivores   **herbivores**   **producers**   **consumers**   (1)

(b)   An animal that only eats plants is a

secondary consumer   **top carnivore**   **primary consumer**   **producer**   (1)

Q2   A biologist is studying a coastal ecosystem. She draws the food chain below.

plankton $\longrightarrow$ shrimp $\longrightarrow$ herring $\longrightarrow$ seagull

(a)   Give the definition of an ecosystem.

....

....   (1)

(b)   Name the tertiary consumer in this food chain.

....   (1)

The biologist wants to draw a food web for the coastal ecosystem.

(c)   Give one difference between a food chain and a food web.

....

....   (1)

(d)   Here is some more information about organisms in the coastal ecosystem.

> Shrimps can be eaten by crabs.
> Herrings can be eaten by seals.
> Both seals and seagulls eat crabs.

Use this information and the food chain above to draw a food web for the coastal ecosystem.

(3)

Q3 A food web is shown.

(a) The organisms in this food web are interdependent. Explain what is meant by the term 'interdependent'.

....

....

.... (1)

(b) Write down the food chain that includes the weasel.

.... (1)

(c) Suggest what might happen to the number of rabbits if the amount of grass increased. Explain your answer.

Result: ....

Explanation: .... (1)

(d) (i) Explain what might happen to the number of owls if all the hawks die.

....

.... (1)

(ii) Explain what might happen to the number of frogs if all the hawks die.

....

.... (1)

(e) A disease kills all the mice. Explain one reason why the number of squirrels might increase and one reason why the number of squirrels might decrease.

....

....

....

....

....

....

.... (4)

Score: [ ] out of **17**

Section B3 — Interactions and Interdependencies

Population Size

Q1 Lions and hyenas share the same habitat in Africa.
They compete with each other to survive.

(a) Suggest one resource that lions
and hyenas might compete for.

.... (1)

(b) Lions and hyenas are predators. Explain what this means.

.... (1)

(c) Lions' prey includes antelopes. Explain what might happen to the antelope
population if the population size of the lions increased.

....

.... (1)

Q2 A student is estimating the number of buttercups in his garden.

He uses the piece of equipment shown on the right.

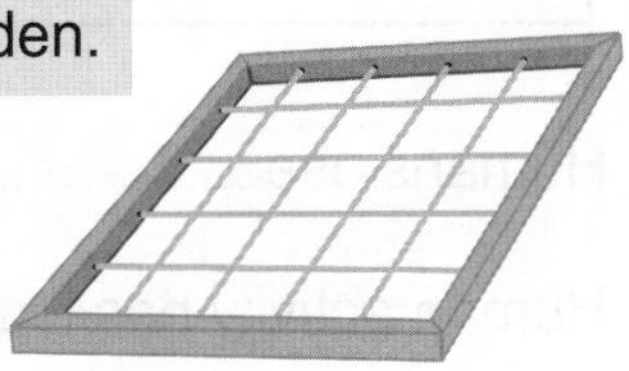

(a) Name this piece of equipment.

.... (1)

The student places this piece of equipment at five random sample points in his garden.
He counts the number of buttercups inside the frame at each point.
His results are shown in this table.

Sample point	1	2	3	4	5
Number of buttercups	12	8	9	4	7

(b) Calculate the mean number of buttercups.

No. of buttercups = ... (2)

(c) The student works out that his garden has an area of 32 m².
The frame he used had an area of 1 m².
Calculate an estimate of the size of the population of buttercups in the garden.

Population size = ... (1)

Score: ☐ out of **7**

Protecting Living Things

Q1 Orang-utans live in the Indonesian rainforest.
They mostly eat fruit and leaves from the trees.

(a) A company wants to cut down a large area of rainforest in Indonesia.
Explain how this could affect the population size of the orang-utans.

....

....

.... (2)

(b) Use the words in the box to complete the paragraph below.
Each word may only be used once. You will not need to use all the words.

increasing	pollution	environment	conserving
living	generations	decreasing	habitats
sustainable	resources	organism	population

Humans use .... from the Earth to survive.

Human activity has led to .... of the environment and

damage to many .... The human population is

.... So we need to manage the way we use resources

to meet our needs without destroying things for future ....

— this is called .... development. (6)

Q2 The Arabian oryx is hunted for its horns. In 1972 there were no longer any Arabian oryx in the wild. Due to conservation work, there are now wild populations again.

(a) Some Arabian oryx are kept in captivity in zoos.
Explain how a zoo could help to conserve the wild Arabian oryx population.

....

.... (2)

(b) Suggest another conservation scheme that could be used to protect the oryx.

.... (1)

Score:		out of **11**

Variation

Q1 The graph on the right shows the number of people who have each different blood group in a population.

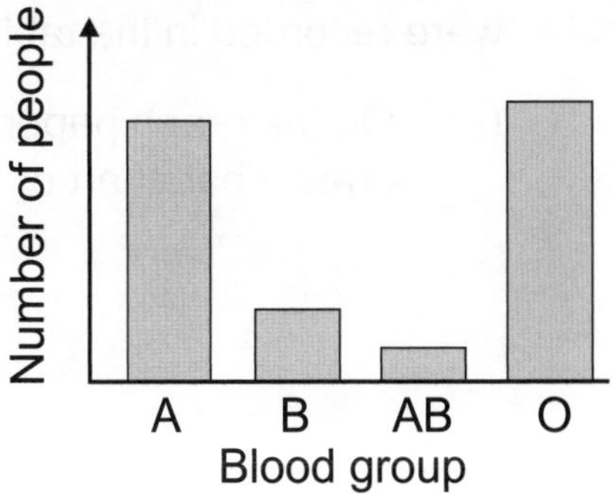

State whether the variation shown by the graph is continuous or discontinuous. Explain your answer.

Type of variation: ....

Explanation: ....

.... (1)

Q2 Humans and gorillas are different species.

Human    Gorilla

(a) State two similarities between humans and gorillas.

1. ....

2. .... (2)

(b) There are also differences between the two species.
   (i) Using the photos above, describe two differences between humans and gorillas.

   1. ....

   ....

   2. ....

   .... (2)

   (ii) Explain why these differences occur.

   ....

   .... (1)

Q3 Eye colour and height show variation in humans.

The eye colours of the students in two Year 7 classes were recorded in the table on the right.

Eye colour	Number of students
Blue	7
Brown	37
Green	12
Other	4

(a)   On the graph paper below, draw a bar chart of the results.

(3)

(b)   A student wants to investigate the height variation in her class.

Suggest two things the student should do to make sure the height measurements she takes are accurate. Explain your reasoning for each point.

1. ....

....

....

2. ....

....

....   (4)

(c)   Height is an example of a quantity showing continuous variation.
Give three more examples of continuous variation in living things.

1. ....

2. ....

3. ....   (3)

Score: ☐ out of **16**

Inherited and Environmental Variation

Q1 Variation can be inherited or be a result of the environment.

(a) Underline an example of inherited variation from the options below.

scars   **weight**   **eye colour**   **hair length**   (1)

(b) Underline an example of variation from the options below that is only a result of the environment.

blood group   **language**   **skin colour**   **foot length**   (1)

Q2 Anton and Marcus are identical twins. They have an older sister called Isobel.

(a) Both Anton and Marcus have a small, rounded nose. Isobel has a straight, pointed nose. State whether this is an example of inherited or environmental variation.

.... (1)

(b) Anton weighs 2 kg more than Marcus.
(i) State whether this is an example of inherited or environmental variation.

.... (1)

(ii) Suggest a reason for this variation.

.... (1)

Q3 In a courgette growing competition, courgette A is measured at 36 cm long and courgette B is measured at 28 cm long.

(a) Suggest three possible causes for this variation.

1. ....

2. ....

3. ....   (3)

(b) Jeff wants to investigate how one of the possible causes of variation affects the length of courgettes. Explain why he must keep all of the other factors that could cause variation the same in his investigation.

....

....

.... (2)

Score: ☐ out of **10**

Classification

Q1 Underline the group of vertebrates that has each of the following characteristics.

    (a) Lay eggs on land, have feathers and wings and are warm-blooded.

        mammals   **birds**   **reptiles**   **fish**   (1)

    (b) Lay eggs in water, have smooth moist skin and are cold-blooded.

        birds   **reptiles**   **fish**   **amphibians**   (1)

Q2 Arthropods A and B are shown on the right.

    (a) Describe the characteristic features of arthropods.

    ....

    ....

    ....   (3)

    (b) (i) Name the group that arthropod B belongs to.

        ....   (1)

        (ii) State one feature of arthropod B that allows you to identify the group it belongs to.

        ....   (1)

Q3 Living things are divided into five kingdoms.

    (a) Describe the differences between the characteristic features of the plant and animal kingdoms.

    ....

    ....   (2)

    (b) Explain why fungi are not included in the same kingdom as plants.

    ....

    ....   (1)

    (c) Single-celled organisms are divided into the Monera and Protista kingdoms. Describe how monerans and protists differ from each other.

    ....   (1)

Score: out of **11**

Using Keys

Q1 The specimens below belong to different groups.

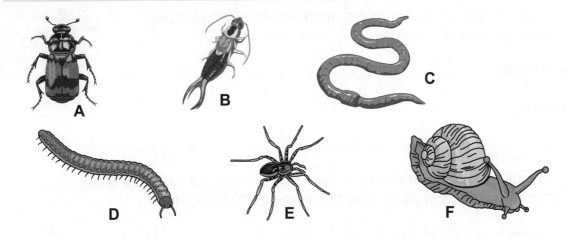

1) Has it got legs?	YES — go to question 2
	NO — go to question 6
2) Has it got 8 legs?	YES — it's an <u>araneae</u>.
	NO — go to question 3
3) Has it got 6 legs?	YES — go to question 4
	NO — go to question 5
4) Has it got a forked tail?	YES — it's a <u>dermaptera</u>.
	NO — it's a <u>coleoptera</u>.
5) Does it look like it has a tail?	YES — it's a <u>scolopendromorpha</u>.
	NO — it's a <u>spirobolida</u>.
6) Does it have a shell?	YES — it's an <u>achatinoidea</u>.
	NO — it's a <u>megadrilacea</u>.

Use the key above to identify the following specimens.

A: ....

B: ....

C: ....

D: ....

E: ....

F: ....   (6)

Score: [   ] out of **6**

The Particle Model

Q1   Solids, liquids and gases can be represented using the particle model.

(a)   Name the state of matter that is represented by the particles shown on the right.   Explain your reasoning.

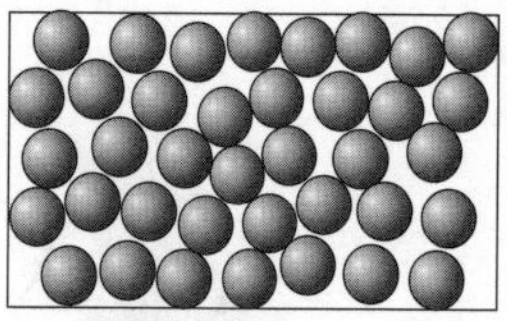

State of matter: ....

Reasoning: ....

....   (2)

(b)   In terms of the particle model, explain why solids keep a definite shape, whereas liquids and gases take the shape of their container.

....

....

....

....   (4)

Q2   The diagram below shows two sealed syringes.
Each syringe contains the same volume of air or water.

Syringe A   seal↓   air   Syringe B   plunger↓   water

(a)   Assume that air and water particles are the same size.
State which syringe contains the larger number of particles.   Explain your answer.

....

....   (2)

(b)   (i)   Suggest a way of increasing the volume of the air in syringe A without changing the number of air particles.

....   (1)

(ii)   Suggest whether it would be possible to increase the volume of the water in a similar way.   Explain your answer.

....

....   (1)

Score: [   ] out of **10**

More on The Particle Model

Q1 Inflatable mattresses are filled with air. The air particles create a gas pressure within the mattress.

(a) Describe how the air particles create pressure in the mattress.

....

.... (1)

(b) Suggest what will happen to the pressure in the mattress if more air is pumped into it. Explain your answer.

....

....

....

.... (2)

Q2 Ena was investigating whether the rate of diffusion in a liquid depends on the temperature of the liquid.

She set up an experiment as shown below.

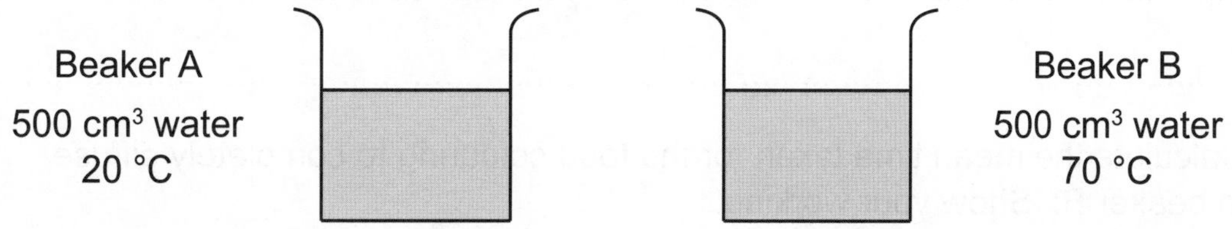

Beaker A
500 cm³ water
20 °C

Beaker B
500 cm³ water
70 °C

5 cm³ of food colouring was added to beaker A and beaker B using a pipette dropper.

Ena then timed how long it took for the food colouring to completely diffuse through the water.

She then repeated the experiment two more times.

(a) Explain what is meant by the diffusion of food colouring in terms of particles.

....

....

.... (2)

(b) Diffusion of food colouring is caused by the Brownian motion of particles. Explain what is meant by Brownian motion.

....

....

.... (2)

Section C1 — The Particulate Nature of Matter

(c) For the experiment outlined on the previous page, underline:

(i) the independent variable

| water temperature | time taken for food colouring to diffuse | volume of food colouring | rate of diffusion | (1) |

(ii) the dependent variable

| water temperature | time taken for food colouring to diffuse | volume of food colouring | rate of diffusion | (1) |

(iii) a control variable

| water temperature | time taken for food colouring to diffuse | volume of food colouring | rate of diffusion | (1) |

The results of the experiment are shown below.

Beaker	Time (s)			
	Experiment 1	Experiment 2	Experiment 3	Mean
A	279	251	232	254
B	108	134	127	

(d) Repeating the experiment three times and taking a mean can improve the precision of the results. Describe two other ways in which the results can be improved by repeating the experiment.

1. ....

2. .... (2)

(e) Calculate the mean time taken for the food colouring to completely diffuse in beaker B. Show your working.

Time = ... s   (1)

(f) Use the results to write a conclusion for this experiment.

....

.... (2)

(g) Suggest one improvement Ena could make to her method to further investigate the relationship between temperature and the rate of diffusion.

....

.... (1)

Score: ☐ out of **16**

Changes of State

Q1 A substance can change state between a solid, a liquid and a gas.

(a) Name the changes of state that are labelled A - D in the diagram below.

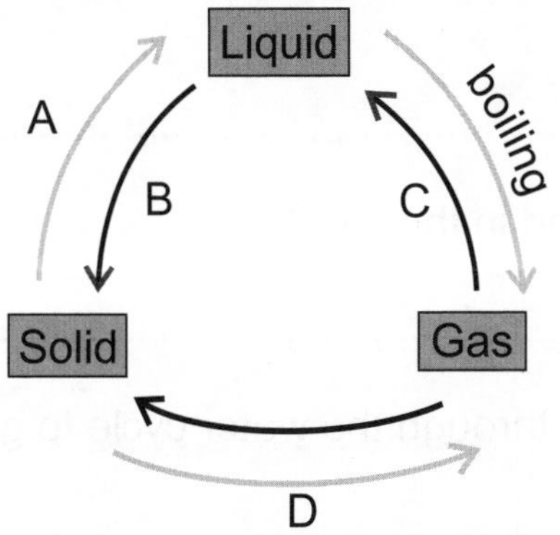

A: .... (1)

B: .... (1)

C: .... (1)

D: .... (1)

(b) A substance can change state from a liquid to a gas by boiling or evaporation. Describe how evaporation differs from boiling.

....

....

.... (2)

Q2 A thin tube of liquid ethanol can be used in thermometers to mark temperatures of up to 78 °C, the boiling point of ethanol.

(a) (i) Describe what happens to the particles of ethanol as its temperature increases.

....

.... (2)

(ii) Explain your answer to part (i).

....

....

.... (2)

(b) Explain how the effect of temperature on the particles of ethanol allows an ethanol thermometer to work.

....

....

.... (2)

Score: [   ] out of **12**

Water

Q1 Water can be found in a solid, liquid or gaseous form on Earth.
It is constantly transferred between these forms through the water cycle.

(a) (i) State a source of solid water in nature.

.... (1)

(ii) Name the gaseous form of water that is found in the air.

.... (1)

(b) Describe the path a water molecule could take through the water cycle to get from an ocean to a lake.

....

....

.... (3)

Q2 Ali is planning a lab experiment to investigate the conditions that affect evaporation rate.

Her method is as follows:

1. Fill two shallow dishes with 500 cm³ of water.
2. Place the dishes in separate cupboards, one with the door closed and one with the door open slightly to create a draft.
3. Measure how much water evaporates from each dish over the course of one day.

(a) Write a prediction for Ali's experiment.

....

.... (1)

(b) Describe how Ali could measure the amount of water that evaporates during the day.

....

.... (1)

(c) Explain why Ali should measure the temperature of both cupboards during the day.

....

....

.... (3)

Score: [   ] out of **10**

Atoms and Elements

Q1 Underline the correct option to complete the sentences below.

    (a)   Different elements contain...

        ...the same type of atom.

        ...the same type of compound.

        ...different types of atom.

        ...different types of compound.   (1)

    (b)   The elements are organised in the

elemental table   **daltonic table**   **chemical table**   **periodic table**   (1)

Q2 Give the chemical symbol of each of the following elements.

    (a)   carbon

    ....   (1)

    (b)   chlorine

    ....   (1)

    (c)   calcium

    ....   (1)

    (d)   copper

    ....   (1)

    (e)   iron

    ....   (1)

Q3 All matter is made up of atoms.

    (a)   Describe what an atom is.

    ....   (1)

    (b)   Describe what an element is.

    ....

    ....   (1)

Score: out of **9**

Compounds

Q1 The particles in four different substances are shown below.

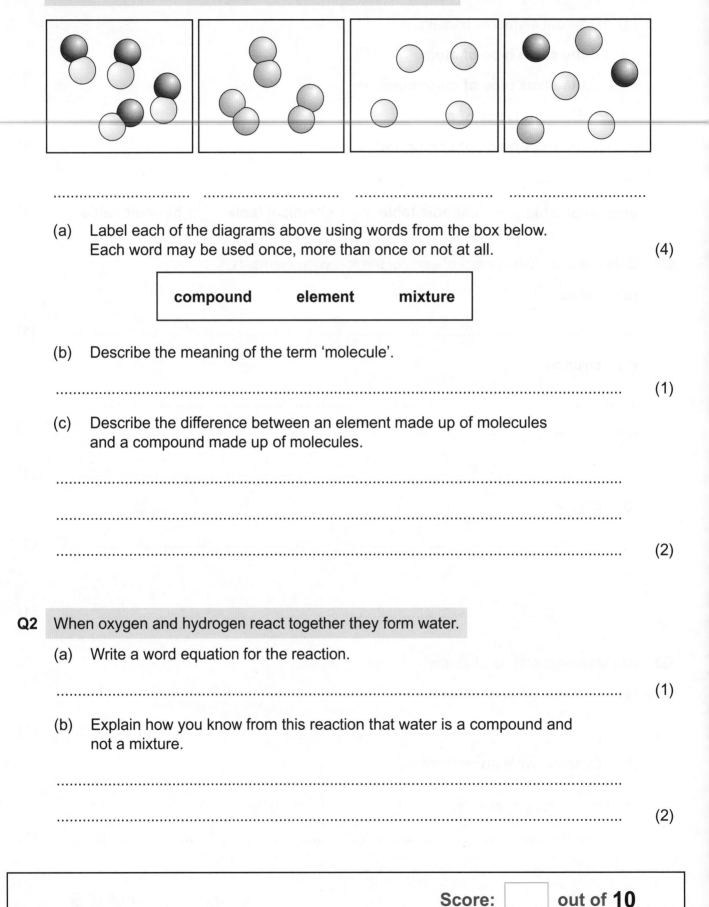

....

(a) Label each of the diagrams above using words from the box below.
Each word may be used once, more than once or not at all. (4)

> **compound** **element** **mixture**

(b) Describe the meaning of the term 'molecule'.

.... (1)

(c) Describe the difference between an element made up of molecules
and a compound made up of molecules.

....

....

.... (2)

Q2 When oxygen and hydrogen react together they form water.

(a) Write a word equation for the reaction.

.... (1)

(b) Explain how you know from this reaction that water is a compound and
not a mixture.

....

.... (2)

Score: ☐ out of **10**

Chemical Formulae

Q1 Give the chemical formulae of the following compounds.

(a) carbon dioxide

.... (1)

(b) sodium hydroxide

.... (1)

(c) sulfuric acid

.... (1)

Q2 Three substances are shown below. The diagrams include the chemical symbols of the elements in each substance.

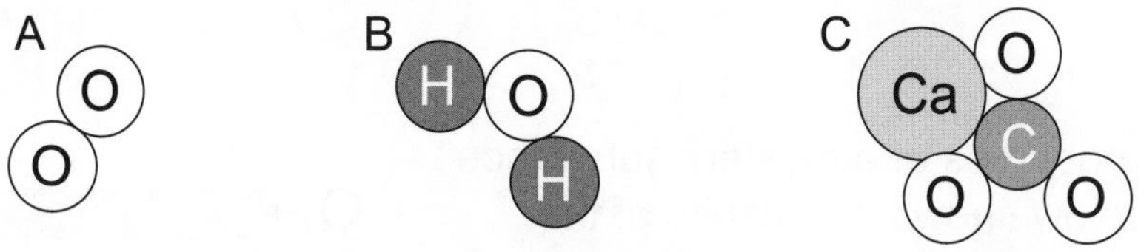

A
O
O

B
H O
H

C
Ca O
C
O O

State the name of each of these substances.

A: ....

B: ....

C: .... (3)

Q3 State the name of the compound formed from the following reactants.

(a) sodium and chlorine

.... (1)

(b) copper, oxygen and sulfur

.... (1)

Q4 A compound is made up of one carbon atom and four hydrogen atoms.

(a) Write the chemical formula of this compound.

.... (1)

(b) Name this compound.

.... (1)

Score: [   ] out of **10**

Properties of Metals and Non-Metals

Q1 Complete the sentences below by underlining the best option.

(a) An example of a basic oxide is

carbon dioxide   **sulfur dioxide**

magnesium oxide   **nitrogen dioxide**   (1)

(b) Sulfur dioxide can be added to water to form a solution with a pH of

2   **7**   **9**   **14**   (1)

(c) An element that you would expect to be a solid at room temperature is

nitrogen   **chlorine**   **zinc**   **neon**   (1)

Q2 John investigated the properties of a mystery substance called "Q". The table below shows the results of the tests (A – D) that he did on the substance.

Q →

Test	Description of Test	Result
A	Attach Q in an electric circuit with a light bulb	No light
B	Bend Q	Cracks appear
C	Hold Q in a Bunsen burner flame	Starts to melt
D	Hold Q near a bar magnet	No attraction

(a) State whether substance Q is a metal or a non-metal.

.... (1)

(b) Name the physical property that is being tested in test B.

.... (1)

(c) Explain the result of test A.

....

....

.... (2)

Section C2 — Atoms, Elements and Compounds

Q3 Layla has three different samples of substances.

> Sample 1 is a dull red colour. It's an electrical insulator and has a low melting point.
>
> Sample 2 is a shiny brownish orange colour. It has a high melting point and can be hammered into sheets.
>
> Sample 3 shatters when dropped on the floor. It isn't magnetic and has a low boiling point.

(a) Give the sample(s) that are non-metals.

.... (1)

(b) Give the sample(s) that are metals.

.... (1)

(c) State whether you would expect sample 2 to be an electrical conductor or an electrical insulator. Explain your answer.

....

....

.... (2)

Q4 Saucepans are normally made out of metal.

(a) Describe one property of metals that makes them suitable materials for saucepans.

....

....

.... (2)

(b) Some saucepans have a handle made out of non-metal. Explain why a person may prefer to use a saucepan like this.

....

....

.... (3)

Score: [ ] out of **16**

Purity and Mixtures

Q1   Becky reads several reliable sources that tell her
the melting point of pure citric acid is 153 °C.

(a)   Underline the option below that completes the following sentence.

A pure substance is always made up of...

...particles of only one element.

...particles of only one element or one compound.

...particles of only one compound.

...particles of two or more compounds.   (1)

(b)   Becky's teacher gives her a sample of citric acid which is a white solid.
She tests the melting point of the solid and finds that it is 148 °C.
Suggest why the melting point of Becky's sample isn't 153 °C.

....

....   (1)

Q2   Jack added 25 g of sugar to 100 g of water in a beaker.
He stirred it until the sugar had completely dissolved.

(a)   State which substance is the solvent in Jack's solution.

....   (1)

(b)   State which substance is the solute in Jack's solution.

....   (1)

(c)   Calculate the total mass of Jack's solution.

Mass = ... g   (1)

(d)   Describe what happens to the molecules of sugar when the sugar
dissolves in the water. In your answer, you should include a description
of how the sugar particles are distributed within the water.

....

....

....

....   (3)

Q3 Air is a mixture of gases.

(a) State what is meant by the term mixture.

....

.... (1)

(b) The pie chart below shows the composition of the air.

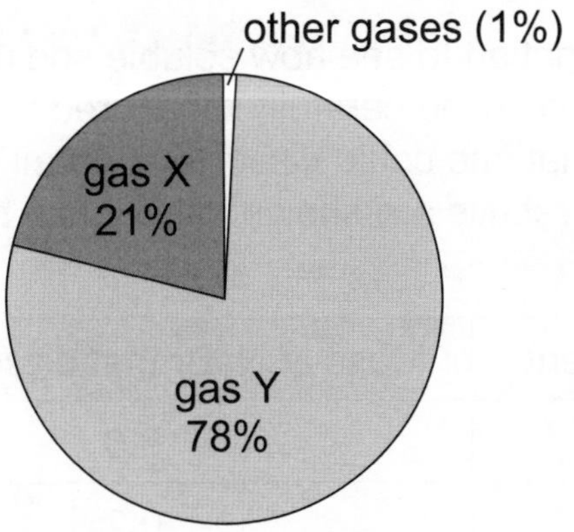

other gases (1%)

gas X
21%

gas Y
78%

(i) Name gas X.

.... (1)

(ii) Name gas Y.

.... (1)

(iii) Name one of the other gases that is found in air.

.... (1)

(iv) Name the gas found in air that is an important reactant in respiration.

.... (1)

Q4 You can make a salt solution by dissolving solid sodium chloride in water.

(a) State whether this process is a chemical change or a physical change.

.... (1)

(b) A small dish of salt solution was left in a warm room for a week. Predict how the contents of the dish would look at the end of the week. Explain your answer.

Prediction: ....

Explanation: ....

.... (3)

Score: ☐ out of **17**

Solvents and Solutions

Q1 Underline the solvent below that is an important solvent in the human body.

ethanol   **propanol**   **water**   **propanone**   (1)

Q2 Zara carried out an investigation to see how soluble sodium bromide (NaBr) is in different solvents. She carefully measured the maximum mass of sodium bromide that she could dissolve in 10 ml of solvent at room temperature. Her results are shown in the table below.

Name of solvent	Mass of NaBr that dissolved (g)
water	9.0
ethanol	0.2
methanol	1.5

(a) The solutions that Zara produced were saturated.
Explain what is meant by the term saturated solution.

.... (1)

(b) (i) Name the independent variable in Zara's investigation.

.... (1)

(ii) Name the dependent variable in Zara's investigation.

.... (1)

(c) State which of the three solvents sodium bromide is most soluble in.
Explain your answer.

Solvent: ....

Explanation: .... (2)

(d) Zara repeats her experiment, but this time she heats the 10 ml samples of the three solvents to a temperature of 30 °C. State whether she will be able to dissolve more or less sodium bromide in the solvents. Explain your answer.

....

.... (1)

Score: ☐ out of **7**

Section C3 — Pure and Impure Substances

More on Water

Q1 Ellen did an experiment to compare the amount of other substances present in seawater, tap water and distilled water. The method that she used is shown in the box below.

> 1. Weigh an empty evaporating dish and record its mass.
> 2. Measure out 30 ml of seawater into the dish.
> 3. Heat the dish gently until all the water has evaporated.
> 4. Weigh the dish again to find the mass of any solids left in the dish.
> 5. Repeat steps 1-4 using tap water, then distilled water.

(a) Explain why Ellen used the same volume of each of the three types of water.

.... (1)

(b) The table below shows the results of Ellen's experiment. Complete the second column of the table to show which type of water was in each dish.

Dish	Type of water	Mass of solid left in dish (g)
1	....	1.06
2	....	0.03
3	....	0.00

(2)

(c) Ellen wants to carry out a different experiment to test the purity of a sample of water. Briefly describe how Ellen could check if the sample of water is pure.

....

.... (2)

Q2 Choose words from the box to complete the passage below.

more	less	increases	decreases

When most substances freeze, their particles get closer together.

This makes the substances .... dense. When water freezes,

the particles get further apart. So ice is .... dense than liquid water.

This means that when you freeze water it .... in volume.

(3)

Score: [   ] out of **8**

Separating Mixtures

Q1 Paul has a mixture made up of solid particles of flour and liquid water. He separates the mixture using filtration.

(a) Give the name for a mixture of solid particles in a liquid.

.... (1)

(b) The diagram below shows the set of equipment that Paul used to separate the mixture. Complete the labels on the diagram using words from the box.

| filtrate | residue | funnel | filter paper |

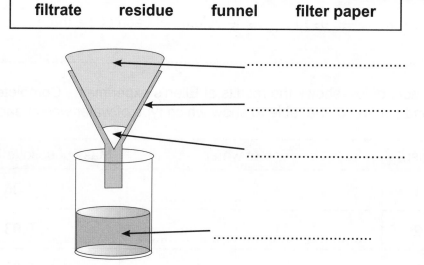

....

....

....

....

(3)

Q2 Tansy used chromatography to separate the dyes in some purple food colouring. The diagram below shows how her experiment was set up and her results.

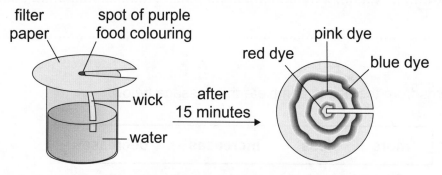

(a) State which colour dye moved through the filter paper the fastest in Tansy's experiment. Explain your answer.

Dye: ....

Reason: .... (2)

(b) Tansy wants to compare her results to the dyes found in other food colourings by carrying out a similar experiment. Name one variable that Tansy should keep constant to ensure her experiment is a fair test.

.... (1)

Q3 Callum has some blackcurrant squash. He uses the apparatus shown below to extract some pure water from the squash.

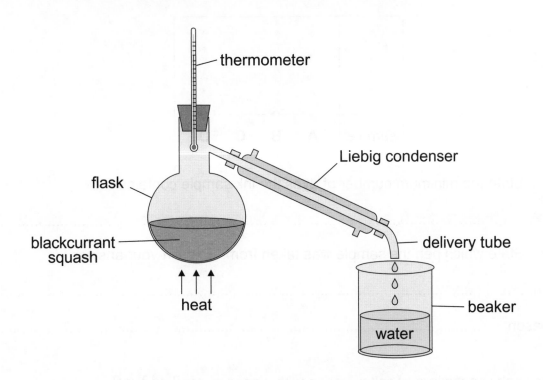

(a) Underline the separation technique that Callum is using.

filtration   **crystallisation**   **distillation**   **evaporation**   (1)

(b) Explain how the Liebig condenser turns the water vapour back into liquid water as it leaves the flask.

....

....

.... (2)

(c) Explain why the end of the delivery tube should not be below the surface of the water in the beaker after the heat has been turned off.

....

.... (1)

(d) Apart from a decrease in volume, state what change you would expect Callum to observe in the liquid in the flask over the course of his experiment. Explain your answer.

Observation: ....

Explanation: ....

.... (2)

Q4 Eve's teacher gave her a sample of some ink from a pen. She used chromatography to work out which one of four pens, **A**, **B**, **C** or **D**, the ink sample was taken from.

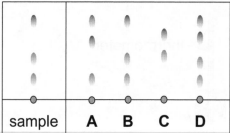

(a) State the minimum number of dyes the ink sample contained.

.... (1)

(b) State which pen the sample was taken from. Explain your answer.

Pen: ....

Reason: .... (2)

Q5 Rock salt is a mixture of salt mixed in with pieces of sand and rock. Describe the method and experimental techniques that you could use to obtain pure salt crystals from a lump of rock salt.

....

....

....

....

....

....

....

....

....

....

....

.... (6)

Score: [   ] out of **22**

Everyday Chemical Reactions

Q1 Tom is doing an experiment which involves heating some chemicals in a test tube. The method tells him to heat the reaction "gently", so he uses a Bunsen burner set to a medium blue flame.

(a) Describe how Tom should set the air hole on a Bunsen burner to get a medium blue flame.

.... (1)

(b) Underline the option that completes the sentence about Bunsen burners below.

Closing the air hole of the Bunsen burner...

...decreases the temperature of the flame because it increases the amount of air entering the burner.

...decreases the temperature of the flame because it decreases the amount of air entering the burner.

...increases the temperature of the flame because it increases the amount of air entering the burner.

...increases the temperature of the flame because it decreases the amount of air entering the burner. (1)

(c) After heating the test tube, Tom sets the Bunsen burner to the safety flame.
(i) What colour is the safety flame?

.... (1)

(ii) Suggest two other safety precautions that Tom should take when he uses a Bunsen burner.

1. ....

2. .... (2)

(d) The diagram below shows the roaring blue flame of a Bunsen burner.

On the diagram, draw a circle around the hottest point of the roaring blue flame. (1)

Q2 When chemical changes occur, new substances are formed.

(a) Underline the example below that is not a chemical change.

a spade rusting   **superglue setting**   **a cake baking**   **ice melting**   (1)

(b) If copper oxide is heated, no chemical change will take place.
Name one other substance that does not change chemically when heated.

....   (1)

Q3 Billie's father tells her that if bananas are placed in a sealed
container, they will ripen more quickly than if left on the counter.
Billie decides to test this. She seals one unripened bunch of bananas
in a container, and leaves another unripened bunch out on the counter.

(a) Suggest what Billie's prediction should be for this experiment.

....

....   (1)

(b) State one control variable in this experiment.

....   (1)

(c) Explain why some variables need to be controlled.

....   (1)

As bananas ripen, they develop brown spots. After three days, Billie opens the container
and removes the bananas. The two bunches of bananas are shown below.

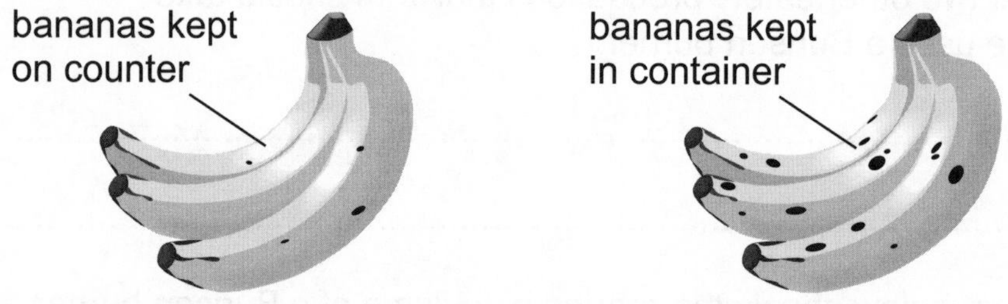

bananas kept
on counter

bananas kept
in container

(d) Write a conclusion for this experiment.

....

....

....

....   (2)

Score: _____ out of **13**

More on Chemical Reactions

Q1 Shanti heats some white lead carbonate powder with a Bunsen burner.
She uses the apparatus below. After a while, the powder turns yellow.

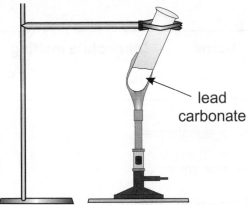

lead
carbonate

(a) Explain how Shanti knows that a chemical change has occurred.

.... (1)

(b) Shanti measures the total mass of the test tube and powder before
and after the reaction. Her results are shown in the table below.

Mass before	Mass after
40.0 g	39.3 g

Calculate the difference in mass.

Difference in mass = ... g   (1)

(c) Suggest why the mass appears to have decreased.

....

.... (1)

(d) Explain why mass is always conserved in a chemical reaction.

....

.... (1)

(e) Shanti is concerned about the effect of random error on her results.
Suggest what she could do to reduce the effect of random error on her results.

....

.... (1)

Score: [   ] out of **5**

Combustion and Oxidation

Q1 Combustion is an oxidation reaction.

(a) Use the words and phrases in the box below to complete the following sentences about combustion.

| a bike rusting | burns | chocolate melting | a bonfire |
| melts | water freezing | freezes | rusts |

Combustion is when a substance ....

in oxygen to release energy.

An example of a combustion reaction is .... **(2)**

(b) Explain why combustion is an oxidation reaction.

.... **(1)**

Q2 Bella uses the apparatus on the right to test whether a candle produces carbon dioxide. Any gas released by the candle will pass through the limewater.

Explain how Bella will know whether carbon dioxide is produced by the candle.

limewater

....

.... **(1)**

Q3 Anan builds a bird table in his garden using iron nails. After two weeks, he observes that the colour of the nails has changed from shiny grey to a dull brown.

(a) Complete the word equation for the reaction that has taken place.

iron + oxygen $\longrightarrow$ .... **(1)**

(b) State the name given to the type of reaction observed by Anan.

.... **(1)**

Q4 The diagram below shows a burning splint.

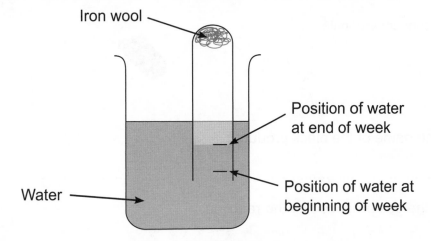

Flame

Wooden splint

(a) Heat and oxygen are required for the splint to continue burning. State the third necessary requirement for the flame to continue burning along the splint.

.... (1)

(b) The flame is blown out so that the splint is just glowing.
Describe how the splint can now be used to test for the presence of oxygen.

.... (1)

Q5 Annie places a piece of iron wool in a test tube and suspends it upside down in water. The diagram below shows the set-up a week later.

Iron wool

Position of water at end of week

Position of water at beginning of week

Water

(a) Explain why the level of water in the test tube has risen.

....

.... (2)

(b) Annie uses the position of the water at the beginning of the week and the end of the week to measure the change in volume of air in the test tube.
She finds the volume of air has decreased from 20 cm^3 to 16 cm^3 during the week.
Using these results, give a conclusion for Annie's experiment.
Include any relevant calculations in your answer.

....

....

....

.... (4)

Score: ☐ out of **14**

Section C4 — Chemical Reactions

Thermal Decomposition Reactions

Q1 When hydrated copper sulfate is heated, it forms anhydrous copper sulfate and water.

(a) State the colour of hydrated copper sulfate.

.... (1)

(b) A student has a sample of anhydrous copper sulfate.
He adds water to the sample. Describe the colour change he would observe.

.... (1)

Q2 A student heated copper carbonate, as shown in the diagram below.
It changed colour from green to black and a gas was given off.

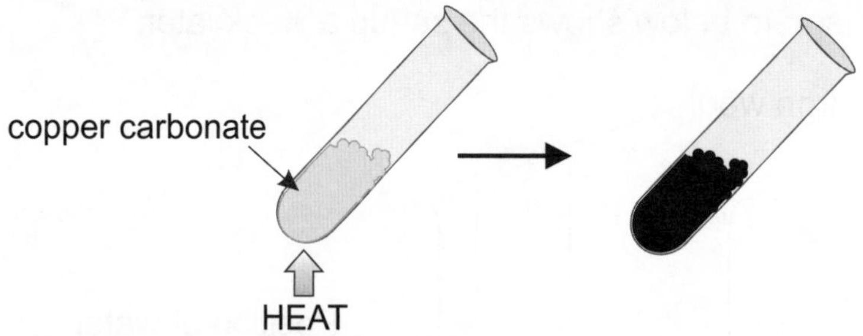

copper carbonate

HEAT

(a) Give the name of the black product.

.... (1)

(b) Name the gas produced by the reaction.

.... (1)

(c) Write a word equation for this reaction.

.... (1)

Q3 A sample of potassium permanganate is heated.

(a) Describe the colour change that takes place when potassium permanganate
is heated.

.... (2)

(b) Name the three products of this reaction.

1. ....

2. ....

3. .... (3)

Score: [   ] out of **10**

Reactivity Series and Metal Extraction

Q1 Most metals are mined from compounds found in the Earth.

(a) Complete the sentences about metal reactivity using the phrases in the box below.

very reactive	combined with other substances	on its own	not very reactive

Gold is found in the ground ....

but sodium is found ....

This is because gold is ....

and sodium is ....   (4)

(b) Give one use for gold based on its reactivity.

....   (1)

(c) Lead is another metal mined from the ground.
Give one use for lead. Explain why lead is suitable for this use.

Use: ....

Explanation: ....

....   (3)

Q2 A reactivity series lists elements in order of their reactivity.

(a) Place the elements from the box into the correct places in the reactivity series below.

copper	magnesium	sodium

Most reactive: Potassium

                    ....

                    ....

                    Carbon

                    ....

Least reactive: Silver   (2)

(b) State the element listed in part (a) that is a non-metal.

....   (1)

Q3 Misty owns a chainsaw with an iron chain. She leaves the chainsaw outside. After a week, she discovers that the chain has started to rust.

(a)   Explain why the chain has started to rust.

.... (1)

Misty buys a new chain. She decides to oil the chain to prevent it from rusting.

(b)   Explain why oiling is a suitable method for protecting an iron chain from rusting.

....

.... (2)

(c)   State one other way to protect iron from rusting.

.... (1)

Q4 Some metals can be extracted from their ores using carbon.

(a)   Tick the correct box for each metal in the table below to show which metals can be extracted from their ore using carbon.

Metal	Extracted using carbon?	
	Yes	No
zinc		
potassium		
lead		
calcium		
magnesium		

(5)

(b)   Iron can be extracted from iron oxide using carbon.
Write the word equation for the reaction between iron oxide and carbon.

.... (1)

(c)   Explain why aluminium can't be extracted from its oxide using carbon.

.... (1)

Score: [   ] out of **22**

Reactions of Metals with Oxygen and Water

Q1 Callum investigated the reactivity of three unknown metals — A, B and C. He set up three test tubes, each containing a sample of one of the metals. He then added some water to each test tube and recorded whether a reaction took place. If a reaction didn't take place, he tested the metal to see if it would react with steam. His results are shown below.

Test tube	Metal	Reaction with water?	Reaction with steam?
1	A	yes	-
2	B	no	no
3	C	no	yes

water

sample of metal

(a) Put the metals above in order from most to least reactive.

Most reactive   Least reactive

.... , ... , ...   (1)

(b) A gas was produced by the reaction in test tube 1. State the name of this gas.

....   (1)

(c) Callum wants to investigate the reactivity of metals A, B and C with oxygen. Write a prediction for this investigation.

....

....   (1)

Q2 Rayna is investigating the reactions of different metals with oxygen.

(a) State what type of reaction this is.

....   (1)

(b) Underline the correct word to complete the sentence below.

Most metals react with oxygen to form a metal...

   ...carbonate.   **...oxide.**   **...hydroxide.**   **...sulfate.**   (1)

(c) Rayna heats samples of lead, silver, zinc and calcium in oxygen. Suggest which of these metals would give the most violent reaction with oxygen. Explain your answer.

Metal: ....

Explanation: ....   (2)

Score: ☐   out of **7**

Displacement Reactions

Q1 When brown iron oxide is heated with grey aluminium powder, a reaction occurs and a white powder and a lump of metal are formed.

(a) Explain what is happening during the reaction to give these products.

....

.... (2)

(b) Suggest the identity of the white powder.

.... (1)

Q2 A student wanted to compare the reactivity of four different metals — magnesium, copper, zinc and a mystery metal X. The student added a piece of each metal to test tubes filled with zinc sulfate solution and left them for half an hour.

magnesium   copper   zinc   metal X

zinc sulfate solution

(a) Give two control variables for this experiment.

1. ....

2. .... (2)

After half an hour, the student observed that in the test tube containing magnesium, zinc metal had been deposited on the magnesium strip. No reaction had occurred in the other test tubes.

(b) Complete the word equation below to show what happened in the test tube with the strip of magnesium.

magnesium + zinc sulfate → .... + ... (1)

The student then tested metal X and zinc in copper sulfate solution.
Copper metal was deposited in both test tubes.

(c) Using the student's results, write the metals used in the experiment in order of reactivity, from the most reactive to the least. Include metal X in your answer.

.... (1)

Score: [   ] out of **7**

Acids and Alkalis

Q1 Jan tested some substances around her home with Universal indicator solution.

Her results are shown in the table below.

Substance	Universal indicator colour
Lemon juice	Red
Drain cleaner	Purple
Washing up liquid	Blue
Rain water	Yellow

(a) Name the substance in the table that is a strong alkali.

.... (1)

(b) Suggest the pH value of lemon juice.

.... (1)

(c) Jan wants to know if vinegar is an acid. Other than using Universal indicator, suggest a method that she could use to test for acidity.

....

.... (2)

Q2 Alan wants to know the pH of the soil in his garden. He takes soil samples from six randomly chosen points in his garden and tests the pH.

His results are shown in the table below.

Sample site	1	2	3	4	5	6
Soil pH	7.2	7.8	7.0	7.7	8.0	8.5

(a) Calculate the mean (average) pH of the soil samples.

Mean pH = ... (1)

(b) Explain why the soil sample sites were chosen at random.

.... (1)

(c) Suggest one thing that Alan could do to improve the repeatability of his results.

.... (1)

(d) Alan wants to plant some flowers that prefer a slightly acidic soil.
Predict whether these flowers will grow well in his garden. Explain your answer.

....

.... (1)

Score: ☐ out of **8**

Neutralisation

Q1 Zhen wants to make some salts using neutralisation reactions.

(a) State what acid she could use to produce each of the salts below.

copper sulfate: ....

sodium nitrate: ....

zinc chloride: .... (3)

(b) Zhen reacts copper oxide with the appropriate acid to make copper sulfate.
Name the other product formed by this reaction.

.... (1)

Q2 A salt solution can be made by neutralising sodium hydroxide with hydrochloric acid. The method for this reaction is shown below.

> 1. Add 1 cm^3 of hydrochloric acid to a test tube containing 20 cm^3 of sodium hydroxide.
> 2. Remove a small sample of the solution in the test tube and check to see if the pH is neutral.
> 3. Repeat this process until you have a neutral solution.

(a) Name an indicator that would be suitable to use to check the pH.

.... (1)

(b) Name the salt formed during this reaction.

.... (1)

(c) Suggest one safety precaution you should take when working with acids and alkalis.

.... (1)

(d) Kevin decides to carry out this experiment, but adds 5 cm^3 of acid in step 1, rather than 1 cm^3. He measures the pH with a digital pH meter and records his results in the table below.

Volume of acid added (cm^3)	0	5	10	15	20
pH of solution	13.0	13.0	12.5	12.0	5.0

Explain why Kevin cannot use the resulting solution to produce a pure sample of salt.

....

....

.... (3)

Q3 When a metal carbonate reacts with an acid a salt is formed.

(a) Complete the word equation below to show all the products formed when a metal carbonate reacts with an acid.

metal carbonate + acid →

salt + ... + ... (2)

(b) Name the salt formed during the reaction between calcium carbonate and sulfuric acid.

.... (1)

(c) Calcium carbonate is a base. Describe what is meant by the term base.

....

.... (1)

Q4 Mia makes a salt solution by reacting hydrochloric acid with potassium hydroxide.

(a) Name the salt in the salt solution.

.... (1)

The following pieces of equipment are available for Mia to use.

Bunsen
burner

evaporating
dish

tripod and
gauze

(b) Outline a method that Mia could use to produce large salt crystals from the solution using the equipment above.

....

....

....

.... (3)

Score: ☐ out of **18**

Reaction of Metals with Acids

Q1 Josh put some aluminium in a flask with some dilute hydrochloric acid.
He collected the gas produced by the reaction and recorded the total volume
of gas given off at regular intervals. His results are shown in the table below.

Time (s)	Volume of gas (cm³)
0	0
10	1.6
20	2.8
30	3.6
40	4.0
50	4.0

(a) Draw a graph of his results on the grid below. Include a curved line of best fit.

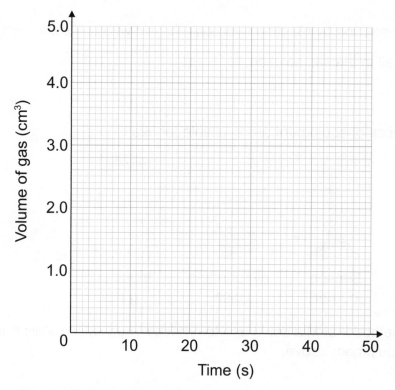

(2)

(b) (i) Name the gas produced by this reaction.

.... (1)

(ii) Josh holds a lighted splint to the mouth of a test tube that contains
the collected gas. Describe what the result of this test should be.

.... (1)

(c) As well as the gas, another product was formed in the reaction. Name this product.

.... (1)

Section C4 — Chemical Reactions

The apparatus Josh used is shown below.

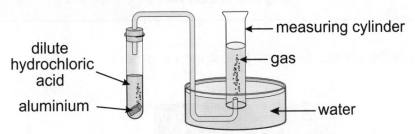

The more vigorously a metal and acid react, the faster the rate of gas production.

(d)   Josh wants to put together a reactivity series using five metals. Describe how Josh could use his set-up to find out the reactivity of the different metals.

....

....   (2)

Q2 A student tested the reaction of four unknown metals (labelled A, B, C and D) with dilute hydrochloric acid. She set up four test tubes as shown on the right and recorded her observations of the reactions that occurred.

dilute hydrochloric acid

metal

The student's results are shown in the table below.

Metal	Observations of reaction
A	Bubbled slightly
B	Bubbled vigorously
C	Bubbled slightly
D	No reaction

(a)   The student took steps to make sure she could compare the reactions fairly. Suggest two steps she may have taken.

1. ....

2. ....   (2)

(b)   State which of the metals is most likely to be copper. Explain your answer.

Metal: ....

Reason: ....   (2)

(c)   The other three metals were magnesium, iron and zinc.
State which of the metals is most likely to be magnesium. Explain your answer.

Metal: ....

Reason: ....   (2)

Score: [   ]   **out of 13**

Section C4 — Chemical Reactions

Limestone

Q1 The photograph below shows a natural limestone pavement.

(a) Give the name of the main compound that makes up limestone.

.... (1)

(b) Blocks of limestone can be used to construct buildings.
   (i) Suggest a disadvantage of constructing buildings out of limestone.

   .... (1)

   (ii) Give two other uses of limestone in the construction of buildings.

   1. ....

   2. .... (2)

(c) Limestone will react with dilute hydrochloric acid.
   Underline the compound below that is not produced by this reaction.

   water   **calcium oxide**   **carbon dioxide**   **calcium chloride**   (1)

Q2 Agricultural lime can be applied to fields to alter the pH of the soil.

(a) (i) State the effect agricultural lime has on soil pH.

   .... (1)

   (ii) Name the type of reaction that causes this effect.

   .... (1)

(b) Describe how agricultural lime is produced.

   ....

   .... (2)

Score: [   ] out of **9**

Acids and the Environment

Q1 Rain water is naturally acidic.

(a) Name the gas that dissolves in rain water to make carbonic acid.

.... (1)

(b) There are other gases in the atmosphere which contribute to acid rain.
Name one of these gases.

.... (1)

(c) George wants to buy a statue for his garden but he is concerned about
damage from acid rain. He has a choice of the four statues shown below.

A   B   C   D

Limestone   Copper   Iron   Magnesium

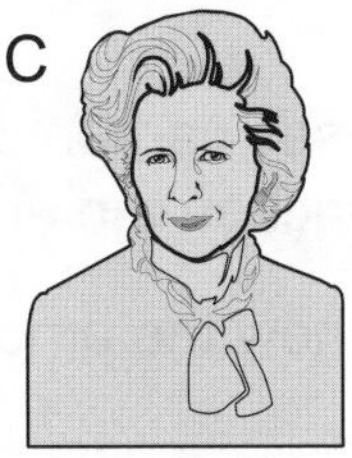

State which statue is the least likely to be affected by acid rain. Explain your answer.

Statue: ....

Explanation: ....

....

....

....

.... (4)

Q2 Marble is a type of rock that contains calcium carbonate. Some gravestones are made
out of marble. Over time, acid rain wears away the carved lettering on the graves.

(a) Name the process of acid rain wearing away rock.

.... (1)

(b) There is more damage to gravestones caused by acid rain in large cities
compared to small villages. Suggest a reason for this.

.... (1)

Score: [ ] out of **8**

The Effects of Fossil Fuels

Q1 Fossil fuels can be burnt in air.

(a) Complete the word equation below to describe the complete combustion of a fossil fuel.

fossil fuel + ... → water + carbon dioxide

(1)

(b) Give two other products that are released if the fuel doesn't burn completely.

1. ....

2. .... (2)

Q2 Burning fossil fuels releases carbon dioxide and can have a negative impact on the environment.

The graph below shows how the amount of carbon dioxide in the atmosphere has changed over time.

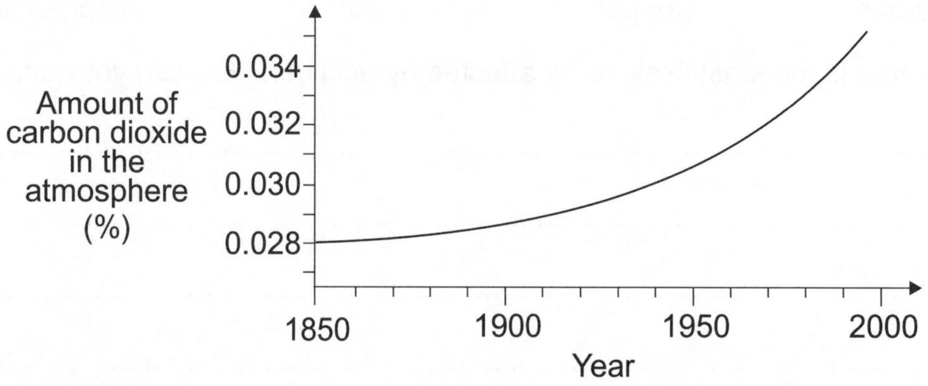

(a) Describe the trend in the amount of carbon dioxide in the atmosphere shown by the graph.

.... (1)

(b) Keisha thinks that the average global temperature will have increased over the same time period. Explain why she might think this.

....

.... (2)

(c) Suggest one way we can reduce the level of carbon dioxide in the atmosphere.

.... (1)

Score: out of **7**

Section C4 — Chemical Reactions

Energy Transfer

Q1 Underline the form of energy that is in each of the following examples.

(a) A sandwich.

chemical   **kinetic**   **elastic**   **light**   (1)

(b) A stretched rubber band.

elastic   **electrical**   **light**   **chemical**   (1)

(c) A complete circuit with a current flowing through it.

light   **gravitational potential**   **elastic**   **electrical**   (1)

Q2 Describe the main energy transformations taking place in each of the following examples.

(a) Releasing a stretched spring.

.... (2)

(b) A coal fire burning.

.... (2)

(c) A current flowing through an electric buzzer.

.... (2)

Q3 A pulley is used to lift a piano to the first floor of a building. The higher the piano is lifted, the more energy it stores.

(a) Name the form of energy that the piano stores.

.... (1)

(b) The piano is accidentally dropped and falls to the ground. Describe the main energy transformations that take place as:
(i) the piano falls,

....

.... (1)

(ii) the piano hits the ground.

....

.... (1)

Score: ☐ out of **12**

Conservation of Energy

Q1   The diagram shows the amount of energy given out by a television in five minutes.

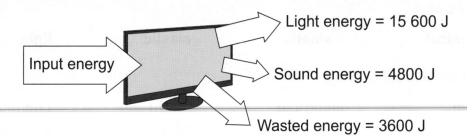

Light energy = 15 600 J

Input energy

Sound energy = 4800 J

Wasted energy = 3600 J

Underline the input energy that the television is supplied with in five minutes.

7200 J	**19 200 J**	**20 400 J**	**24 000 J**

(1)

Q2   State the Law of Conservation of Energy.

....

....   (1)

Q3   Charlotte connects a battery to a light bulb in an electrical circuit. All of the chemical energy supplied by the battery is transformed to electrical energy in the circuit. Some of it is then transformed into light energy in the bulb. 12 J of energy is supplied by the battery and 3 J is transformed into light energy.

(a)   Calculate the amount of energy wasted.

Energy wasted = ... J   (1)

(b)   Charlotte notices that the light bulb warms up whilst the bulb is on.
Explain why this is, in terms of energy transfers by the bulb.

....

....

....   (2)

(c)   Charlotte knows that if she rubs her hands together then they warm up.
She says that this happens because energy has been created.
Explain why Charlotte is incorrect.

....

....   (1)

Score: ☐ out of **6**

Energy Resources

Q1 The following chains show how energy from the Sun is transferred to different energy resources. Underline the word that correctly fills the gap in each chain.

(a) Sun's energy to food:

Sun ⟶ light energy ⟶ .... ⟶ photosynthesis ⟶ food

plants　　　　**animals**　　　　**biomass**　　　　**dead plants**

(1)

(b) Sun's energy to wave power:

Sun ⟶ .... ⟶ causes wind ⟶ causes waves

light energy　　**heats atmosphere**　　**photosynthesis**　　**cools sea**

(1)

Q2 Use words and phrases given to fill in the gaps in the passage below to explain how the Sun drives the water cycle. You don't have to use all the words and phrases, but each word or phrase can only be used once.

sublimate	**freeze**	**snow**
evaporate	**cools down**	**condense**	**clouds**
hail	**heats up**	**boil**

The Sun warms up water in seas, lakes and rivers, causing it to ....

and turn into water vapour. As the water vapour rises it .... ,

causing it to .... into lots of tiny droplets of liquid water

— otherwise known as clouds. The water can then fall to the ground again as rain,

.... , or ....

(5)

Q3 Batteries are used to store energy obtained from other energy resources.

(a) State the form of energy stored in batteries.

.... (1)

(b) State how this energy can be released from batteries.

.... (1)

Q4 Biomass is an example of an energy resource that relies on plants using photosynthesis to capture and store the Sun's energy.

(a) Give one example of biomass.

.... (1)

(b) Name two energy resources that do not rely on photosynthesis to form.

1. ....

2. .... (2)

Q5 Fossil fuels are currently the main energy resources used by humans.

(a) Name the three fossil fuels.

.... (3)

(b) Describe how energy from the Sun ends up in fossil fuels.

....

....

....

.... (4)

(c) State how energy can be released from fossil fuels.

.... (1)

Q6 Wind power is one energy resource that uses the wind to generate electricity.

(a) Explain how the Sun creates wind on Earth.

....

....

....

.... (3)

(b) Apart from wind power, name one other energy resource that relies on wind.

.... (1)

Score: ☐ out of **24**

Generating Electricity

Q1 Underline the energy resource that doesn't require a turbine to generate electricity.

wave power   **coal**   **wind power**   **solar power**   (1)

Q2 Underline the option that completes the sentence below.

Electricity is generated from wave power by...

...waves pushing air in and out of a turbine.

...water continuously flowing through a turbine.

...waves pushing air in and out of a generator.

...water continuously flowing through a generator.   (1)

Q3 An energy company currently uses coal to generate their electricity.
They would like to start using wind power to generate some of their electricity.

(a) Describe how coal can be used to generate electricity.

....

....

....

....

....

....

....   (4)

(b) Describe how wind turbines are used to generate electricity.

....

....   (2)

(c) The energy company has two possible locations where wind turbines could be built.
Location A is at the top of a hill and Location B is in a valley.
Suggest which location would be better for building wind turbines. Explain why.

....

....   (1)

Score: ☐ out of **9**

Renewable and Non-Renewable Energy Resources

Q1 Energy resources can be described as either renewable or non-renewable.

(a) Describe the difference between renewable and non-renewable energy resources.

....

.... (1)

(b) Give two examples of a non-renewable energy resource.

1. ....

2. .... (2)

(c) Give three examples of a renewable energy resource.

1. ....

2. ....

3. .... (3)

Q2 Sophie lives in a country where coal is the most used energy resource. Sophie suggests the government should build solar panels in her town to increase the amount of renewable energy resources used by the country.

Discuss the advantages and disadvantages of Sophie's suggestion.

....

....

....

....

....

....

....

....

....

.... (6)

Score: ☐ out of **12**

Speed

Q1 An aeroplane flies a total distance of 6600 miles when flying from London to Tokyo. The flight lasts 12 hours. Calculate the average speed of the aeroplane.

Speed = ... mph   (1)

Q2 Chris and Jenny went to the same beach, but they got there in different ways.

(a) Jenny took 1000 s to reach the beach and walked 900 m to get there. Calculate the speed she was travelling at in m/s. Show your working.

Speed = ... m/s   (1)

(b) Chris drove 10 km to the beach at a speed of 40 km/h. Calculate how long it took him to get to the beach in hours. Show your working.

Time = ... hours   (2)

Q3 A horse trainer wants to compare the speeds of two different horses.

(a) Describe a method she can use to calculate the average speeds of the horses as they run round a 1 km race track.

....

....

....

....   (2)

(b) State how the trainer can make her results repeatable.

....   (1)

(c) State how the trainer can make sure the investigation is a fair test.

....

....   (1)

Score: _____ out of **8**

More on Speed

Q1 A car moves past a school bus on the opposite side of a road.

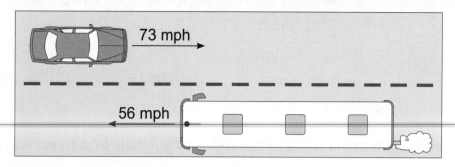

73 mph

56 mph

Calculate the speed of the car relative to the bus.

Speed = ... mph   (2)

Q2 The graph below shows the distance of a remote control helicopter from the ground against time.

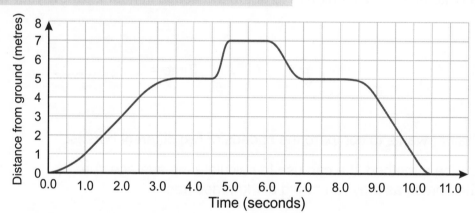

(a) Describe the motion of the helicopter between 9.0 and 10.0 s.

....

....   (2)

(b) Calculate the speed of the helicopter between 1.0 and 2.5 s.

Speed = ... m/s   (2)

(c) State the time at which the helicopter is moving fastest.

Time = ... s   (1)

Score: ☐ out of **7**

Forces

Q1 Forces can't be seen, but their effects can be.

(a) State what is meant by a force.

.... (1)

(b) (i) State the S.I. unit of force.

.... (1)

(ii) Name a device that can be used to measure force.

.... (1)

(c) Applying a force to an object can cause it to speed up or start moving.
State two other effects that applying a force can have on an object.

1. ....

2. .... (2)

Q2 The parachute on a drag racing car travelling at a steady speed opens,
causing a drag force to act in the opposite direction to the car's motion.
Write down the main effect of this force on the movement of the car.

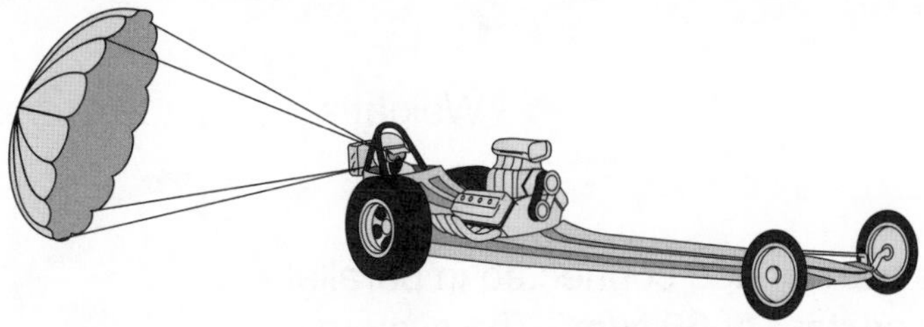

.... (1)

Q3 The diagram below shows a car driving along a road. The arrow shows the force
from the engine. The friction acting on the car is equal to the force from the engine.
Draw a second arrow onto the diagram to show the friction acting on the car.

force from engine

(2)

Score: [   ] out of **8**

Springs

Q1 Springs obey Hooke's Law.

(a) State Hooke's Law.

....

.... (1)

(b) A spring has a spring constant of 60 N/m.
Calculate the force needed to extend it by 0.1 m.

Force = ... N   (1)

Q2 A toy bird is suspended at rest from a spring with a spring constant of 25 N/m.

(a) State the direction of the force exerted by the bird on the spring.

.... (1)

(b) When the bird is removed from the spring, the spring compresses
back by 20 cm. Calculate the weight of the toy bird.

Weight = ... N   (1)

Q3 The diagram below shows two springs connected in parallel.
Each spring has a spring constant of 60 N/m. The system
is supported at the top and the bottom is pulled down with a
force of 9.0 N. Calculate the extension of the spring system.

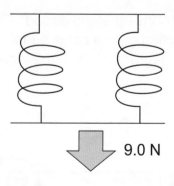

9.0 N

Extension = ... m   (2)

Q4 Manny is hanging blocks of different weights from a spring and measuring the spring's extension.

(a) (i) State the independent variable in this experiment.

.... (1)

(ii) State the dependent variable in this experiment.

.... (1)

Manny's results are shown below. The table is incomplete.

| Weight (N) | Extension (cm) | | | |
	Reading One	Reading Two	Reading Three	Mean
0.1	0.9	1.0	0.8	0.9
0.2	1.9	1.9	1.9	1.9
0.3	2.7	2.3	2.5	2.5
0.4	3.6	3.9	3.6	
0.5	4.5	4.6	4.4	

(b) Complete the final column of the table. (2)

(c) (i) On the graph below, plot the data from the table and draw a line of best fit. Make sure you include a sensible scale for each axis.

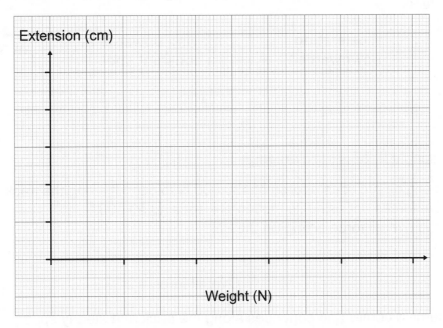

(3)

(ii) Use your graph to predict the weight required to extend the spring by 3.5 cm.

Weight = ... N (1)

Score: ☐ out of **14**

Balanced and Unbalanced Forces

Q1 For each sentence below, underline the option that best completes it.

(a) The diagram below shows the forces acting on a shark.

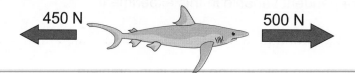

450 N   500 N

The shark is

speeding up   **slowing down**   **travelling at constant speed**   **at rest**   (1)

(b) The diagram below shows the forces acting on a helicopter.

25 000 N

300 N   22 000 N

The helicopter is

accelerating upwards   **accelerating downwards**   **moving upwards at a constant speed**   **at rest**   (1)

Q2 A train moving along a track is accelerating.

(a) The train's engine provides a force of 130 000 N to push it along the track.
The resistive forces opposing its motion are equal to 50 000 N.
Calculate the overall force acting on the train.

Overall force = ... N   (1)

(b) The train turns a corner and continues along the track at a steady speed.
Describe the forces acting on the train as it travels at a steady speed.

....

....   (1)

Q3 Emma suspends a weight from a spring. The weight is at rest.

(a) Underline the options that complete the sentence below.

The spring and the weight are in **motion** / **equilibrium** and the forces on

each object are **balanced** / **unbalanced** .   (1)

(b) Emma pulls downwards on the weight so that the total downwards force on the weight is 5.5 N. The upwards force acting on the weight is 3.0 N. Calculate the overall force acting on the weight.

Overall force = ... N   (1)

Q4 A cherry is placed on a cake. There are two forces acting on the cherry — an upward force from the cake's frosting and the downward force of the cherry's weight.

(a) State what will happen to the cherry if the two forces are balanced.

....   (1)

(b) State what will happen to the cherry if its weight is larger than the force from the frosting.

....   (1)

Q5 A car is travelling forwards along a road.

The diagram below shows the horizontal forces acting on the car.

7000 N

6000 N

1000 N

(a) Explain whether the forces acting on the car are balanced or unbalanced.

....

....   (1)

(b) The driver increases the driving force until the forces on the car are balanced. Describe the motion of the car when the forces are balanced.

....   (1)

Score:		out of **10**

Section P2 — Motion and Forces

Friction and Resistance

Q1 An ice skater skates across an ice rink.

(a) State what is meant by friction.

....

.... (1)

(b) Friction acts between the ice skates and the ice.
(i) Describe one way in which this friction is an advantage when skating.

....

.... (1)

(ii) Describe one way in which this friction is a disadvantage when skating.

....

.... (1)

Q2 A skydiver jumps out of a plane.

(a) The skydiver can adjust his posture as he is falling to make his body more streamlined. Explain what will happen to his falling speed if he does this.

....

.... (2)

(b) Describe how the air resistance acting on the skydiver changes with the skydiver's speed.

.... (1)

(c) Explain why the skydiver reaches a steady falling speed after deploying his parachute.

....

.... (1)

Q3 Aroosa makes a small parachute for a weight by suspending the weight from a square of thin plastic material with some thread.

square of thin plastic material

thread

weight

(a) Aroosa wants to find out how the area of the parachute affects the drag it provides to the weight when it is dropped. Write an experimental method Aroosa could carry out to investigate this.

....

....

....

....

....

....

....

....

....

....

....

.... (6)

(b) Explain why Aroosa should repeat any measurements she carries out.

.... (1)

(c) Suggest the purpose of suspending a weight from the parachute instead of simply dropping each parachute by itself.

....

.... (1)

(d) Suggest what the results from this experiment will show. Explain your answer.

....

....

.... (2)

Score: [   ] out of **17**

Section P2 — Motion and Forces

Stopping Distances

Q1 The stopping distance of a car is affected by many different factors.

(a) Name two factors that affect the stopping distance of a car.

1. ....

2. .... (2)

(b) Two identical cars are racing along a track.
Car A is travelling at 57 mph and car B is travelling at 52 mph when a piece of debris falls onto the track. The drivers both apply the same braking force until their cars come to a stop. Explain which car is likely to have a greater stopping distance.

.... (1)

Q2 In Britain, measures are taken by the government and local councils to improve road safety.

(a) (i) 20 mph speed limits are often enforced on the roads around schools. Explain how this helps to reduce the risk of accidents.

....

....

....

.... (2)

(ii) Suggest why the roads around schools are suitable places for a 20 mph speed limit.

....

.... (1)

(b) Salt reduces the melting point of ice so that it melts at a lower temperature. Explain how salt spread on icy roads would reduce stopping distance.

....

....

....

.... (2)

Score: [   ] out of **8**

Forces and Rotation

Q1 Underline the option that best completes the sentence below about the following diagram.

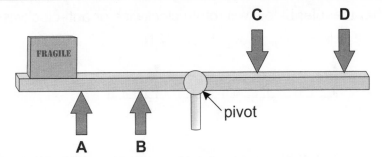

pivot

In order to lift the box with the least effort, the force should be applied at

A   **B**   **C**   **D**   (1)

Q2 A gardening store sells two different wheelbarrows, wheelbarrow A and wheelbarrow B, as shown in the diagram on the right.

Explain which wheelbarrow you would use to carry a very heavy load.

....

....

....

....

....   (2)

Q3 Levers can make it easier to lift and turn objects.

(a) Describe what is meant by a lever.

....

....   (1)

(b) Explain why it is easier to shut a door by pushing near the door handle rather than pushing near to the hinge.

....

....

....   (1)

Score: _____ out of **5**

Moments

Q1 A moment is the turning effect of a force.

(a) Explain whether the ruler below will rotate clockwise or anti-clockwise.

....

....

.... (3)

(b) The 8 N force is moved so that it is now applied at the 2 cm mark on the ruler instead. Explain where on the ruler the 12 N force should be applied for the moments to be balanced.

....

....

.... (3)

Q2 Tito applies a force of 22 N to the handle of a screwdriver to open a can of paint. He uses the edge of the paint can as a pivot.

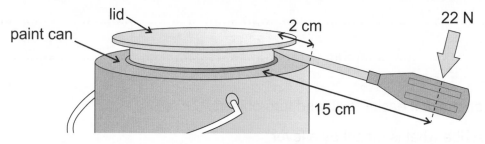

(a) Calculate the clockwise moment about the edge of the paint can.

Clockwise moment = ... Ncm (2)

(b) Calculate the force exerted on the lid.

Force = ... N (2)

Score: ☐ out of **10**

Pressure

Q1 Complete the sentences below by underlining the correct option.

Pressure is calculated using the force applied at an angle of **45°** **90°** to an area.

The greater the area over which the force acts, the **smaller** **greater** the pressure. (1)

Q2 Anne sees a pencil lying on her desk. She manages to balance it on its end.

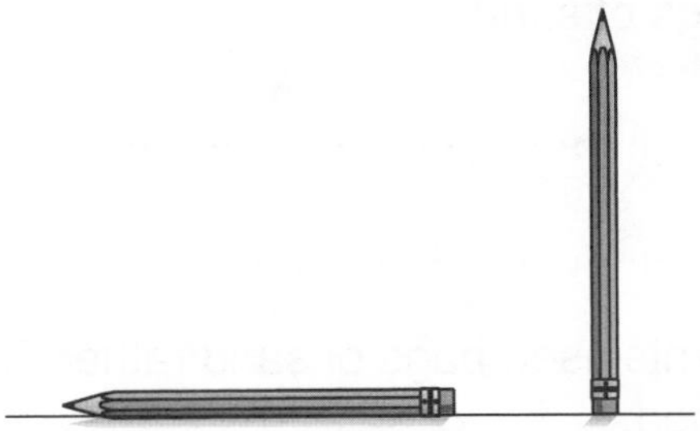

(a) The pencil has a weight of 0.20 N. Each side of the pencil has an area of 2.5 cm². Calculate the pressure exerted by the pencil on the desk when it is lying on its side.

Pressure = ... N/cm² (1)

(b) When the pencil is balanced on its end, it exerts a pressure of 0.4 N/cm² on the desk. Calculate the area of the pencil's end.

Area = ... cm² (2)

Q3 The diagram shows a pair of traditional snowshoes. They are designed to have a large area. In snowy weather, one is attached to the bottom of each shoe to make walking easier. Explain how this works.

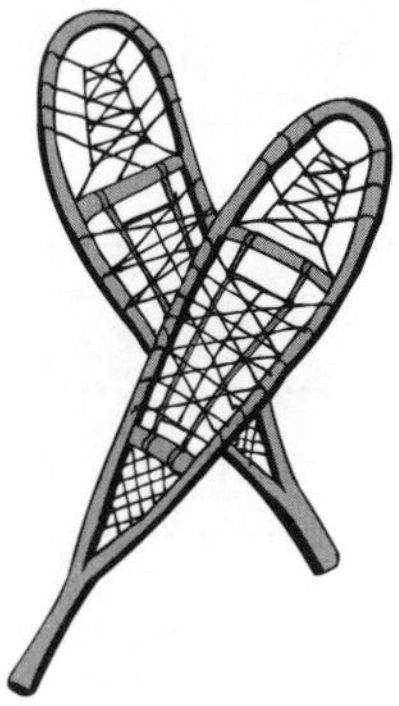

....

....

....

....

.... (3)

Q4 A student drama company is designing a small wooden walkway that is able to support one person. They need to make sure the wood is thick enough to withstand the pressure of someone standing in the centre of it.

Students cut identical lengths of wood of different thicknesses. They support the length at each end and place three bags of sand in the centre. The total weight of the sand is 600 N, which is about the average weight of a human. They record whether or not the wood bends or breaks under the weight.

(a) State the independent variable in this test.

.... (1)

(b) Describe how the students can calculate the pressure exerted on the wood by the bags of sand.

....

.... (1)

(c) Suggest why the students used bags of sand rather than a person to test the wood.

.... (1)

(d) Explain why this method could lead to them using a wood thickness that is too weak to hold a human who weighs 600 N.

....

.... (2)

Q5 The diagram on the right shows a balloon that has been dropped onto a bed of nails. When the same balloon is dropped onto a single nail, it pops. Explain why the balloon pops on a single nail but not on the bed of nails.

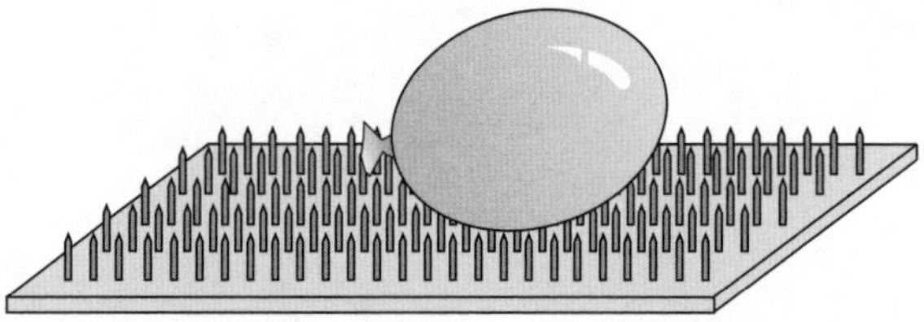

....

....

....

....

.... (3)

Score: ☐ out of **15**

Density

Q1 Xiomara has a cuboid-shaped pendant with rounded edges as shown in the diagram. It is made from glass with a density of 2.5 g/cm³.

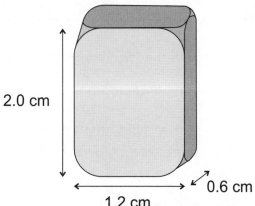

2.0 cm

1.2 cm

0.6 cm

(a) State the relationship between density, volume and mass.

.... (1)

(b) (i) Estimate the volume of the pendant.

Volume = ... cm³ (1)

    (ii) Use your answer from part (b) (i) to estimate the mass of the pendant.

Mass = ... g (2)

(c) She uses a mass balance to find the mass of the pendant.
Explain whether the mass will be higher or lower than your estimate.

....

.... (1)

(d) Describe how Xiomara could use a measuring cylinder and a jug of water
to get a more accurate value for the volume of the pendant.

....

....

....

.... (3)

Q2 Michael is given a container filled with an unknown liquid by his teacher. He is asked to find the density of the liquid. Describe how Michael can find the density of the liquid using a beaker and mass balance.

....

....

....

....

.... (3)

Q3 Gary has an antique spoon. He wants to find out whether it is made from a valuable metal.

He places the spoon into a measuring beaker filled with water. Before inserting the spoon, he notes that the water has a volume of 250.0 cm³. When the spoon is completely submerged in the beaker, the water level rises to 255.0 cm³.

(a) Calculate the volume of the spoon.

Volume = ... cm³ (1)

He looks up the densities of different metals and finds the table below.

Metal	Density / g/cm³
Gold	19.3
Copper	8.9
Brass	8.4 – 8.7

(b) He measures the mass of the spoon to be 45 g. Suggest whether the spoon is most likely to be made from gold, copper or brass. Justify your answer.

....

....

....

.... (2)

Score: [   ] out of **14**

Section P2 — Motion and Forces

Sound

Q1 Sylvia stood a ringing alarm clock on top of a block of foam inside a bell jar. When the air was removed from the bell jar with a vacuum pump, the ringing sound stopped.

(a) Explain why removing the air made the ringing sound stop.

....

....

.... (2)

(b) Sylvia removed the foam and repeated the experiment with the alarm clock resting on the base of the jar. She could still hear the ringing sound even after removing the air from the glass. Explain why.

....

.... (2)

Q2 While sitting at home, Russell hears an explosion from a nearby quarry.

(a) Just before he heard the explosion, he felt a faint vibration in the ground. Explain why he felt vibrations in the ground before he heard the explosion.

....

....

.... (2)

(b) Shortly after he heard the explosion, he heard an echo. Use what you know about the properties of sound and the diagram to explain why.

....

.... (2)

Score: [   ] out of **8**

More on Sound

Q1 Four traces of sound waves with different frequencies are shown below.

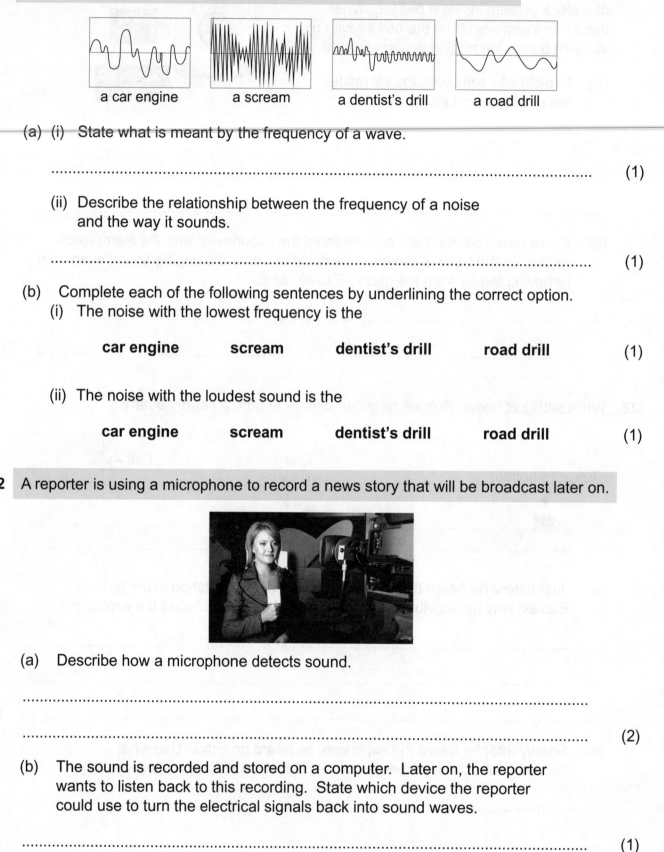

a car engine   a scream   a dentist's drill   a road drill

(a) (i) State what is meant by the frequency of a wave.

.... (1)

(ii) Describe the relationship between the frequency of a noise
and the way it sounds.

.... (1)

(b) Complete each of the following sentences by underlining the correct option.
(i) The noise with the lowest frequency is the

car engine   **scream**   **dentist's drill**   **road drill**   (1)

(ii) The noise with the loudest sound is the

car engine   **scream**   **dentist's drill**   **road drill**   (1)

Q2 A reporter is using a microphone to record a news story that will be broadcast later on.

(a) Describe how a microphone detects sound.

....

.... (2)

(b) The sound is recorded and stored on a computer. Later on, the reporter
wants to listen back to this recording. State which device the reporter
could use to turn the electrical signals back into sound waves.

.... (1)

Score: ☐ out of **7**

Hearing

Q1 The diagram below shows the human ear.

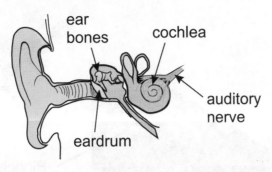

(a) Vibrating hairs in the cochlea turn vibrations into electrical signals that are sent to the brain. Explain how a sound reaching the ear causes the cochlea to vibrate.

....

....

.... (2)

(b) Earplugs are designed to reduce the loudness of any noise that the user is exposed to. Explain why a musician may be advised to wear earplugs at their concerts.

.... (1)

Q2 Matthew is carrying out an experiment to find the highest frequency of sound that people in his class can hear. He sets up a speaker that can play sounds of different frequencies. Each person being tested sits with their back to the speaker and raises their hand every time they hear a sound from it.

(a) Briefly describe what Matthew could do to find the highest frequency sound each person can hear.

....

....

.... (2)

(b) Give two things that should be kept the same for each person to make it a fair test.

1. ....

2. .... (2)

Score: ⬜ out of **7**

Light

Q1 Miranda used a pinhole camera to look at an eagle.

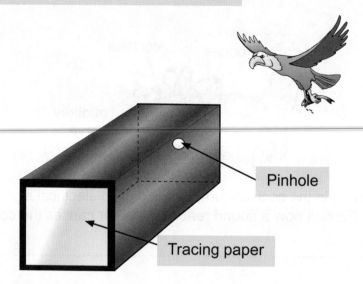

(a) Complete the sentence below by underlining the best option.

The pinhole needs to be small so that

only one ray from each point on the object gets into the camera

the inside of the box is kept very dark

the lens doesn't have to be big

you can only look at the image with one eye (1)

(b) (i) Draw two light rays on the diagram of a pinhole camera below to show how the image of this object is formed.

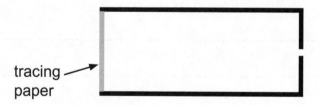

(2)

(ii) Use the diagram you have drawn to explain how an image viewed through a pinhole camera would differ from the object observed.

....

.... (1)

Q2 This question is about sources of light.

(a) State the name given to an object that emits light.

.... (1)

(b) When a star explodes, it can be hundreds of years before
the explosion is observed on Earth. Explain why.

....

....

.... (2)

Q3 Jacques is investigating the speed of sound in a lab. A speaker is placed 30
metres away from a sensor. The speaker produces a short pulse of sound that is
detected by the sensor. The sensor measures time since the pulse was produced
to the nearest hundredth of a second. Jacques writes down how long it took
the sound pulse to reach the sensor and uses this to calculate its speed.

(a) Jacques wants to measure the speed of light. He decides to do the
same experiment, but replace the speaker with a light source and change
the settings of the sensor so that it detects light instead of sound.
Explain the problem with the results that he'll get from this experiment.

....

....

.... (2)

(b) Jacques carries out another experiment. His friend fires a starting pistol from
the other side of a large field. Predict and explain whether Jacques would
hear the gun before, after or at the same time as seeing it fire.

Prediction: ....

Explanation: .... (1)

(c) Explain why light waves can travel through a vacuum but sound waves cannot.
You should use the word particles in your answer.

....

....

....

.... (2)

Score: [ ] out of **12**

Reflection

Q1 Mirrors are able to reflect light.

(a) (i) State what is meant by the normal of a surface.

.... (1)

(ii) State the law of reflection.

.... (1)

(b) A periscope uses mirrors to allow the user to see over obstacles. Add a ray to the diagram on the right to show how the light from the object reaches the user's eye.

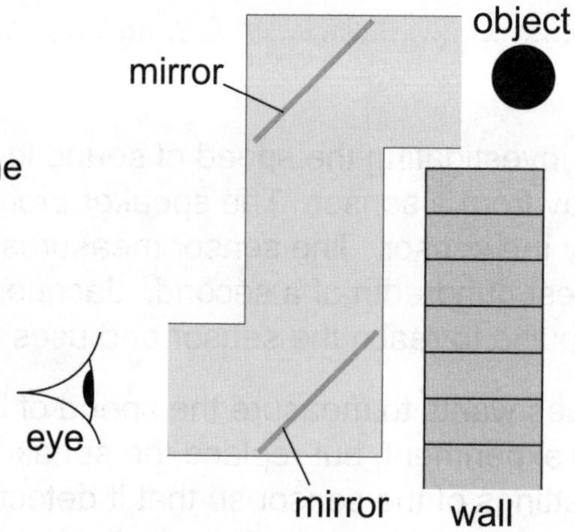

(2)

Q2 A falcon sees a prairie dog ahead of it.

(a) Explain how light rays from the sun allow the falcon to see the prairie dog.

....

....

....

.... (2)

(b) A puddle in front of the prairie dog acts as a plane mirror. State whether or not the prairie dog is able to see the falcon's reflection and justify your answer.

....

....

.... (2)

Score: [   ] out of **8**

Refraction

Q1 A diver uses a torch underwater. The light is visible above the water's surface. Water is denser than air.

(a) Complete the sentence below.

When the light passes from the water to the air at an angle to the normal

it changes .... This is known as .... (1)

(b) A ray of light from the torch travels from the water to the air. In the water the ray of light is travelling along the normal to the surface. State the angle to the normal at which the ray travels through the air after hitting the boundary.

.... (1)

Q2 The angle between a refracted ray of light and the normal is called the angle of refraction.

Ben is given a clear acrylic block, a laser and a piece of paper by his teacher. He places the block on the paper and shines the laser into it. He uses a pencil to draw around the edges of the block and draw the path of the ray onto the paper. The image produced is shown on the right.

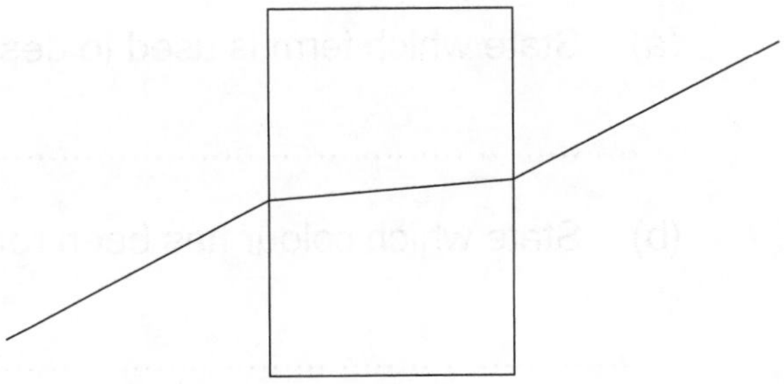

Suggest how Ben can use this method to investigate how the angle of refraction of light passing into the block changes with the angle of incidence.

....

....

....

....

....

....

....

.... (6)

Score: [ ] out of **8**

Transmission and Absorption of Light

Q1 When white light passes through a glass prism it bends and is split up into different colours. A range of colours appears on the screen.

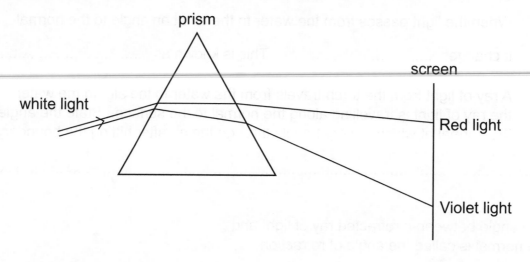

(a) State which term is used to describe the splitting of light into different colours.

.... (1)

(b) State which colour has been refracted the least by the prism.

.... (1)

(c) Explain why white light splits up into different colours when passed through a prism.

....

....

....

.... (3)

(d) Explain why a prism must be transparent to demonstrate this effect.

....

.... (1)

(e) Describe a natural phenomenon in which white light naturally splits into different colours.

....

.... (2)

Q2 Light can be reflected, transmitted or absorbed by objects.

(a) (i) Describe what happens to light when it is shone at a translucent object.

....

.... (1)

(ii) State the name of this effect.

.... (1)

(iii) Complete the following sentence by underlining the correct option.
An example of a translucent material is

water   **tissue paper**   **clear diamond**   **card**   (1)

(b) Complete the following sentence by underlining the correct option.
When light hits an opaque object it is not

reflected   **absorbed**   **transmitted**   **reflected or absorbed**   (1)

(c) (i) Describe what happens to light when it is shone on a transparent object.

.... (1)

(ii) Give one example of a transparent material.

.... (1)

Q3 Oliver decides to investigate how much different colours are refracted by when they are passed into a rectangular glass block.

He shines green, yellow and blue light at the glass block at an angle of 30° to the normal and records the angle to the normal at which each colour travels through the block.

(a) Name the independent variable in this experiment.

.... (1)

(b) Name the dependent variable in this experiment.

.... (1)

(c) Name one control variable in this experiment.

.... (1)

Score: ☐ out of **17**

Electrical Circuits

Q1 The diagram below shows a simple circuit, containing a battery and a bulb.

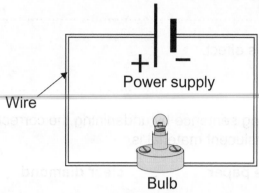

Power supply

Wire

Bulb

(a)   State what is meant by electric current.

.... (1)

(b)   Explain why the bulb lights up.

....

....

.... (2)

(c)   Explain what would happen to the bulb if one of the wires were to be
      replaced by an insulating material.

....

.... (2)

(d)   A second identical bulb is added to the circuit in series.
      (i)   State what happens to the resistance of the circuit.

.... (1)

      (ii) State what happens to the current in the circuit.

.... (1)

      (iii) Explain why both bulbs shine equally brightly.

....

.... (1)

Score: out of **8**

More on Electrical Circuits

Q1 Underline the option that completes the sentence below.

The component above is

    a reed switch   **a push-button switch**   **a relay**   **an SPST**   (1)

Q2 A circuit containing a battery, a bulb and a buzzer is shown below.

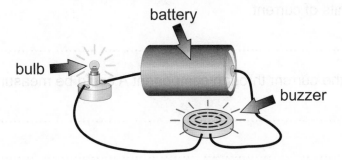

Draw an accurate circuit diagram of this circuit in the space below.

(3)

Q3 Will notices that his battery-powered torch is not as bright as when he first put some batteries in. He thinks that the current supplied by the battery decreases over time. He decides to use a battery, bulb and ammeter connected in series to test this.

(a) State Will's prediction.

.... (1)

(b) Describe an investigation Will could carry out to test his prediction.
Include a description of how he could display his results.

....

....

....

.... (2)

Section P4 — Electricity and Electromagnetism

Q4 The diagram shows a power source connected to a component.

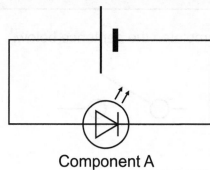

Component A

(a) State the name of component A.

.... (1)

(b) (i) Give the units of current.

.... (1)

(ii) State how the current through component A could be measured.

....

.... (2)

(c) The power supply is prone to power surges in which the current
may get very high. This may cause damage to component A.
Suggest one additional component that should be added to
protect component A from power surges.

.... (1)

Q5 A student puts together a series circuit consisting of a battery, a light dependent
resistor and a motor. She wants to test how the speed of the motor is affected
by the intensity of the light shone on the light dependent resistor.

(a) Complete the circuit diagram below to show the circuit described.

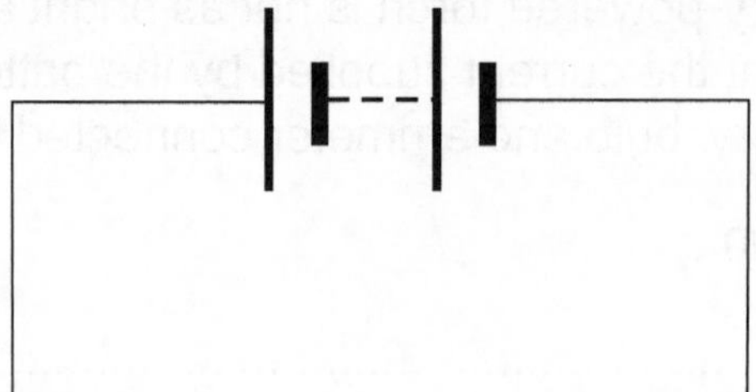

(2)

(b) State the independent variable in the student's experiment.

.... (1)

Score: [   ] out of **15**

Series and Parallel Circuits

Q1 The circuit below has three bulbs.

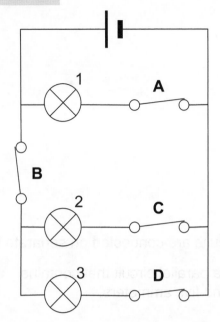

(a) State which of the three bulbs would be lit if only switch A was open.

.... (1)

(b) State which of the three bulbs would be lit if only switch B was open.

.... (1)

Q2 Ammeter A₁ in the circuit below reads 2 A.

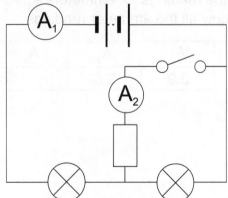

(a) Explain whether the bulbs are in parallel or series.

....
.... (1)

(b) State the current recorded at ammeter A₂, and explain your answer.

....
.... (1)

Q3 In the space below, sketch a simple battery-powered circuit that allows a bulb and a buzzer to be switched on and off independently of each other.

(4)

Q4 Components in parallel circuits are connected on separate loops of wire.

The diagram below shows a parallel circuit that contains a cell, two bulbs, a motor and five ammeters.

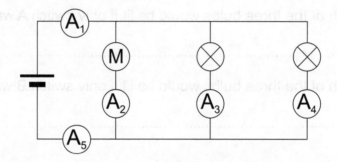

(a) The table below shows the readings for ammeters A_1, A_2 and A_3. Complete the table to show all the ammeter readings.

Ammeter	A_1	A_2	A_3	A_4	A_5
Reading (A)	9.2	3.9	2.6		

(2)

(b) Explain why it is sensible to wire the lights in a house in parallel.

....

.... (1)

Score: [   ] out of **11**

AND and OR Circuits

Q1 The truth table below is for a circuit consisting of one bulb, a battery and two switches.

Input		Output
Switch 1	**Switch 2**	**Bulb**
F	F	F
T	F	F
F	T	F
T	T	T

Explain whether this is an AND circuit or an OR circuit.

....

.... (1)

Q2 The circuit below contains two switches and a bulb.

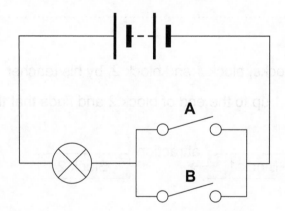

Fill in the output column for the bulb in the truth table below.

Input		Output
Switch A	**Switch B**	**Bulb**
F	F	
T	F	
F	T	
T	T	

(4)

Score: [   ] out of **5**

Magnets

Q1 A compass contains a bar magnet.

(a) State what is meant by a magnetic field.

.... (1)

(b) Sketch the field lines around the bar magnet below to illustrate its magnetic field.

$$\boxed{\text{N} \qquad \text{S}}$$

(2)

(c) Explain why a compass points North.

....

....

.... (2)

Q2 Bertie is given two grey blocks, block 1 and block 2, by his teacher.

He holds the end of block 1 up to the end of block 2 and finds that they attract each other.

attraction

$\boxed{\text{Block 1}} \rightarrow \quad \leftarrow \boxed{\text{Block 2}}$

Bertie concludes that either one or both of the blocks is a magnet.

(a) Bertie flips block 2 around and finds that they still attract each other.

attraction

$\boxed{\text{Block 1}} \rightarrow \quad \leftarrow \boxed{\text{Block 2}}$

State what Bertie's conclusion should now be.

.... (1)

(b) Explain how Bertie could find out for sure whether each block is a magnet or not.

....

.... (2)

Q3 Astrid decides to compare the strengths of five different magnets. To do this, one at a time she places each magnet and a paperclip on a surface and moves the paperclip towards the magnet beside a ruler. She measures the distance at which she first feels the pull of the magnet on the paperclip.

(a) State one variable that should remain constant in this experiment.

.... (1)

(b) Suggest how Astrid could make her results more accurate.

....

.... (1)

Astrid records her results in the table below.

Magnet	1	2	3	4	5
Distance (cm)	4.2	0.6	3.1	2.8	2.7

(c) Use the graph paper below to plot the results on an appropriate graph or chart.

(4)

Score: ☐ out of **14**

Electromagnets

Q1 Electromagnets have many useful applications.

(a) Describe how an electromagnet could be constructed from a piece of insulated wire and an iron bar.

....

.... (2)

(b) State the main difference between this type of magnet and a bar magnet.

....

.... (1)

(c) Suggest two ways of increasing the strength of an electromagnet.

1. ....

2. .... (2)

(d) Explain how iron filings can be used to test for the magnetic field of an electromagnet.

....

.... (1)

Q2 The diagram on the right shows a simple relay circuit. The input circuit contains a switch that connects it to a power supply when it is closed.

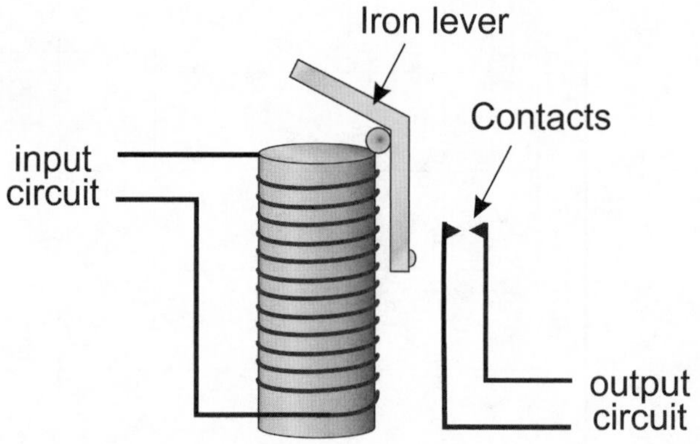

(a) Explain how a relay circuit works.

....

....

....

....

.... (3)

(b) Name one other practical use of electromagnets.

.... (1)

Score: ☐ out of **10**

Gravity

Q1 Complete the paragraph using words from the box below.

attraction	Earth's centre	repulsion
masses	charges	South Pole

There is always a gravitational force of .... between

two .... This means that an object near the

Earth's surface will fall towards the ....

(3)

Q2 Quentin is using a newton meter to measure the weight of a metal disc on Earth. The newton meter and metal disc are shown below.

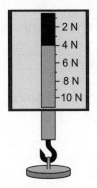

(a) Describe what causes the disc to have a weight on Earth.

....

.... (1)

(b) Using information from the diagram, calculate the mass of the disc.

Mass = ... kg   (3)

(c) Calculate the weight of the disc if it were measured on Mars.
The gravitational field strength on Mars is 3.7 N/kg.

Weight = ... N   (2)

Score: [ ] out of **9**

The Solar System and Beyond

Q1 Our solar system is made up of 8 planets that each orbit around the Sun.

(a) For each of the following, underline the option that best completes the sentence.

(i) The planet that is closest to the Sun is

Venus   **Jupiter**   **Mars**   **Mercury**

(1)

(ii) The galaxy that Earth lies in is called

the Universe   **the Solar System**

Proxima Centauri   **the Milky Way**

(1)

(b) Describe what keeps the planets in orbit around the Sun.

....

....

(2)

(c) Explain why Mars takes longer than Earth to complete one full orbit of the Sun.

....

(1)

(d) Apart from planets, name one other type of object in space that moves in an orbit, and state what it orbits around.

....

(1)

Q2 An astronomer used a telescope to look at some objects in the night sky.

(a) First, he pointed his telescope at Sirius A, a star in our galaxy.
Sirius A is approximately 8.6 light years away from Earth.

Explain what is meant by "8.6 light years".

....

....

(1)

(b) Next, the astronomer pointed his telescope at Jupiter.
Explain why planets such as Jupiter are visible to the astronomer.

....

(1)

Score: [ ] out of **8**

The Movement of the Earth

Q1 The Sun and stars appear to move across the sky over time.

(a) Explain why the Sun appears to move across the sky over the course of a day.

....

.... (1)

(b) At night-time, a star known as the Pole Star appears to remain stationary. The rest of the stars appear to follow a circular path around the Pole Star.

Explain why all of the stars appear to move, and suggest why the Pole Star doesn't.

....

....

.... (2)

Q2 A total lunar eclipse could be seen from the UK on 28th September 2015, whilst a total solar eclipse could be seen from the UK on 11th August 1999.

(a) Describe what is meant by a solar eclipse.

....

....

.... (2)

(b) (i) On the diagram below, draw the relative position of the Sun that would result in a lunar eclipse on Earth. The diagram has not been drawn to scale.

Earth   ● Moon

(1)

(ii) Explain why the Moon is less visible during a lunar eclipse.

....

....

.... (2)

Q3 The diagram below shows the Earth in its orbit during June.
Use the diagram to answer the following questions.

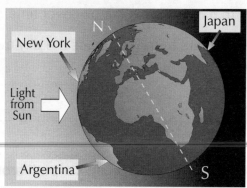

(a) (i) Out of the locations labelled on the diagram, state where it is currently night-time.

.... (1)

(ii) In 12 hours' time, night will become day at this location.
Explain why this change occurs.

....

....

....

.... (2)

(b) It is summer in New York and winter in Argentina during the month of June.
Explain why it is generally warmer in New York than in Argentina in June.

....

....

....

....

....

.... (3)

(c) Describe how the Sun's path across the sky is different in summer
compared to winter.

....

.... (1)

Score: [   ] out of **15**

Satellites

Q1 Underline the option that completes the following sentence about the Moon.

The Moon...

... **is a satellite of the Sun.**

... **is a satellite of the Earth.**

... **is a satellite of Mars.**

... **is not a satellite.**

(1)

Q2 Artificial satellites such as the one shown below are often put into orbit around the Earth.

Give two examples of uses of artificial satellites.

1. ....

....

2. ....

....

(2)

Q3 Since the 1960s, many space probes have been sent to fly by, orbit or land on Mars in order to observe it. However, there has yet to be a manned mission to Mars.

(a) Suggest why probes have been sent to explore Mars instead of manned spacecraft.

....

....

(1)

(b) Suggest what information could be collected with a space probe that would be useful for sending a manned spacecraft to Mars.

....

....

(1)

Score: ☐ **out of 5**

Answers

Section B1 — Structure and Function of Living Organisms

Page 2: Cells

1 a) cell wall: gives support to the cell *[1 mark]*
cell surface membrane: holds the cell together and controls what goes in and out *[1 mark]*
mitochondria: to carry out most of the reactions for aerobic respiration / to release energy for the cell *[1 mark]*
chloroplast: contains chlorophyll and is where the reactions for photosynthesis take place *[1 mark]*

   b) vacuole *[1 mark]*

   c) i) nucleus *[1 mark]*

      ii) They control the production of proteins in the cell *[1 mark]*.

Pages 3-4: More on Cells and Diffusion

1 a) cell — tissue — organ — organism *[1 mark]*

   b) An organ system is a group of organs that work together *[1 mark]*.

2 a) Unicellular means made up of only one cell *[1 mark]*.

   b) i) It helps them to swim *[1 mark]*.

      ii) They allow them to make their own food by photosynthesis *[1 mark]*.

   c) They wrap their cell membrane around the food and take the food into the rest of their body *[1 mark]*.

3 a) cell surface membrane *[1 mark]*

   b) The oxygen molecules will move into the cell by diffusion *[1 mark]* because there is a higher concentration of oxygen molecules outside the cell than inside the cell *[1 mark]*. The carbon dioxide will move out of the cell by diffusion *[1 mark]* because there is a higher concentration of carbon dioxide molecules inside the cell than outside the cell *[1 mark]*.

   c) Glucose molecules will diffuse into the cell *[1 mark]*.

Page 5: The Light Microscope

1 a) E.g. take a small sample of the onion cells and place it in the middle of a clean microscope slide *[1 mark]*. Use a pipette to add a drop of water to the sample *[1 mark]*. Carefully put a clean coverslip over the top *[1 mark]*.

   b) She should be careful not to reflect direct sunlight into the microscope as it could damage her eyes *[1 mark]*.

   c) E.g. select an objective lens (depending on the magnification required) *[1 mark]*. Turn the rough focusing knob to move the objective lens down to just above the slide *[1 mark]*. Then use the fine focusing knob to adjust the focus until a clear image of the cells is visible *[1 mark]*.

   d) methylene blue stain *[1 mark]*

Page 6: Nutrition

1 a) energy *[1 mark]*

   b) growth and repair of tissues *[1 mark]*

   c) energy and insulation *[1 mark]*

2 a)

Food Source	Component
Butter	Lipids
Fish	Proteins
Coffee	Water
Potatoes	Carbohydrates
Salt	Minerals
Carrots	Fibre

[6 marks — 1 mark for each correct answer]

   b) iodine test *[1 mark]*

Page 7: Staying Healthy

1 a) i) mineral *[1 mark]*

      ii) A lack of calcium can lead to osteoporosis / can reduce bone density and make bones more likely to fracture *[1 mark]*.

   b) scurvy *[1 mark]*

2 a) The body doesn't get enough energy and starts to use up its lipid stores *[1 mark]*. This can cause the person to lose weight and feel weak and tired / lead to starvation *[1 mark]*.

   b) i) E.g. high blood pressure *[1 mark]* and heart disease *[1 mark]*

      ii) It can increase your blood cholesterol level, which increases the risk of heart disease *[1 mark]*.

   c) Benedict's solution *[1 mark]*

Pages 8-10: Gas Exchange

1 a) trachea *[1 mark]*

   b) diaphragm *[1 mark]*

   c) i) The volume of the chest increases as the diaphragm moves down *[1 mark]*. This decreases the pressure in the chest, so air rushes in to fill the lungs *[1 mark]*.

      ii) inspiration *[1 mark]*

   d) The diaphragm relaxes/moves up and the external intercostal muscles relax *[1 mark]*. This increases the pressure in the chest, causing air to rush out of the lungs *[1 mark]*.

   e) i) alveoli *[1 mark]*

      ii) Any two from: e.g. they have a large blood supply to carry gases to and away from the lungs. / They have thin walls for gases to diffuse through. / The walls are moist to help gases diffuse through them. *[2 marks — 1 mark for each correct answer]*

2 a) Any two from: e.g. heart disease / (lung) cancer / emphysema *[2 marks — 1 mark for each correct answer]*

   b) It reduces the surface area of the lungs available for diffusion of gases *[1 mark]*, so it can make it difficult for the person to breathe/get enough oxygen *[1 mark]*.

3 a) Point A *[1 mark]*. Exercise causes the heart rate to increase *[1 mark]*.

   b) i) It would have increased *[1 mark]*.

      ii) The cells in Laura's body are respiring more *[1 mark]*, so more oxygen needs to reach the body cells and more carbon dioxide needs to be removed *[1 mark]*.

c) Lung volume increases *[1 mark]*.

4 a) (450 + 525 + 470 + 485 + 415) ÷ 5 = 469 cm³ *[1 mark]*.

b) Taking repeated measurements can improve accuracy *[1 mark]*. It can also make the results more reliable *[1 mark]*.

c) Jackson's results are not precise because they are quite spread out from the mean *[1 mark]*.

d) She needs to take the biggest breath in possible and then measure the total volume of air that she can breathe out *[1 mark]*.

e) The muscles around her bronchioles may contract *[1 mark]* which would narrow her airways *[1 mark]*. The lining of the airways may become inflamed and fluid may build up in the airways *[1 mark]*.

f) Inhalers contain drugs which help to open up the airways *[1 mark]*.

Page 11: Growing Up

1 ovaries *[1 mark]*

2 a)

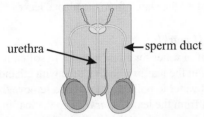

urethra ⟶ ⟵ sperm duct

[2 marks — 1 mark for each correct label]

b) a sex cell *[1 mark]*

c) sperm *[1 mark]*

d) to produce sperm *[1 mark]*

3 a) Any three from: e.g. ovaries start to release eggs. / Ovaries start to produce hormones. / Pubic hair grows. / Hair grows on armpits. / Menstruation starts. / Breasts get larger. / Hips get wider *[3 marks — 1 mark for each correct answer]*.

b) Any three from: e.g. the sex organs get a bit bigger. / Testes start to produce sperm. / Testes start to produce hormones. / Pubic hair grows. / Hair grows on the face, chest and armpits. / Voice deepens. / Shoulders get wider *[3 marks — 1 mark for each correct answer]*.

c) These changes occur so that the body can become able to reproduce *[1 mark]*.

Page 12: The Menstrual Cycle

1 a) i) B *[1 mark]*

ii) A *[1 mark]*

iii) D *[1 mark]*

iv) D *[1 mark]*

b) The lining needs to be thick so that the uterus is ready to receive a fertilised egg *[1 mark]*.

c) 10 days *[1 mark]*

d) Day 14 *[1 mark]*

Pages 13-14: Having a Baby

1 fallopian tube *[1 mark]*

2 a) Sperm are released from the penis into the vagina *[1 mark]*. The sperm then travel to the fallopian tubes where they meet the egg *[1 mark]*.

b) There are millions of sperm and only one egg *[1 mark]*.

c) The head of a sperm breaks through the membrane of the egg cell *[1 mark]*. The nuclei of the sperm and egg cell then fuse together *[1 mark]*.

d) zygote *[1 mark]*

e) The fertilised egg/zygote divides and once it is a ball of cells it's called an embryo *[1 mark]*.

3 When the egg and sperm fuse during fertilisation, the parents' genes mix, so no offspring are identical to either parent *[1 mark]*.

4 a) i) placenta *[1 mark]*

ii) umbilical cord *[1 mark]*

b) gestation *[1 mark]*

c) It protects the fetus from knocks and bumps. *[1 mark]*

d) The placenta lets the blood of the fetus and the blood of the mother get very close together *[1 mark]*. This allows oxygen and nutrients to pass from the mother to the fetus *[1 mark]*. It also allows waste products to be removed from the fetus into the mother's blood *[1 mark]*.

e) Alcohol and nicotine in the mother's blood can pass to the fetus across the placenta *[1 mark]*. They can slow down the development of the fetus and cause a low birth weight *[1 mark]*.

Pages 15-17: Plant Reproduction and Seeds

1 a) i) A *[1 mark]*

ii) F *[1 mark]*

iii) stamen *[1 mark]*

iv) anther *[1 mark]*

b) Insects are attracted to the flower by its coloured petals/ nectar *[1 mark]*. When the insects land on the flower, the pollen sticks to them *[1 mark]*. The insects then carry the pollen to other flowers when they fly away *[1 mark]*.

c) Wind pollination *[1 mark]*. E.g. the flower's filaments may be longer so that the anthers stick outside the flower, so pollen gets blown away from the anthers *[1 mark]*. The flower may also have feathery stigmas to catch the pollen blown from anthers *[1 mark]*.

2 a) Pollination is where pollen grains are transferred from an anther to a stigma *[1 mark]*.

b) fertilisation *[1 mark]*

c) ovary *[1 mark]*

d) Any two from, e.g. embryo root / embryo shoot / seed coat *[2 marks — 1 mark for each correct answer]*.

e) germination *[1 mark]*

3 Tomato: This is animal-dispersed. The fruit is brightly coloured to attract animals to eat it *[1 mark]*.
Dandelion: This is wind-dispersed. It has a parachute so it can catch the wind to be carried away *[1 mark]*.

4 a) Wind dispersal *[1 mark]*

b) i) The distance to which seeds are dispersed *[1 mark]*.

ii) The length/size of the model wings *[1 mark]*

c) i) 30 − 7 = 23 cm *[1 mark]*

ii) E.g. the larger the sycamore fruit the further the fruit is dispersed *[1 mark]*.

d) E.g. by repeating their measurements three times and taking an average *[1 mark]*.

Page 18: Healthy Living

1 All recreational drugs are illegal. *[1 mark]*

2 a) A drug taken for fun *[1 mark]*.

 b) nicotine *[1 mark]*

3 a) Taking drugs that harm your physical or mental health *[1 mark]*.

 b) i) E.g. alcohol is a poison which affects the brain and liver, leading to cirrhosis (liver disease) and other health problems *[1 mark]*. It also impairs judgement, which can lead to accidents *[1 mark]*

 ii) E.g. marijuana can cause hallucinations *[1 mark]*. It can also cause mental health problems, such as anxiety and paranoia *[1 mark]*.

4 Exercise increases the amount of energy used by the body *[1 mark]* and decreases the amount stored as fat *[1 mark]*.

Page 19: Fighting Disease

1 a) i) e.g. colds / flu / chickenpox / German measles *[1 mark]*

 ii) e.g. tetanus / food poisoning / whooping cough *[1 mark]*

 b) Viruses reproduce inside cells and damage them *[1 mark]*. They also release poisons *[1 mark]*.

 c) Bacteria attack body tissues *[1 mark]* or release poisons *[1 mark]*.

2 a) Antibodies to mumps would already have been made by the body, so the body would be ready to fight the infection *[1 mark]*.

 b) E.g. washing hands washes off the microorganisms that cling to our skin when we touch things *[1 mark]*. This stops the microorganisms being passed on to other people *[1 mark]*. Having laws about food preparation helps to prevent harmful microorganisms getting into the food we eat *[1 mark]*.

Section B2 — Material Cycles and Energy

Pages 20-21: Plant Nutrition

1 a) i) water *[1 mark]*

 ii) chlorophyll *[1 mark]*

 b) carbon dioxide + water $\xrightarrow[\text{chlorophyll}]{\text{light energy}}$ glucose + oxygen *[1 mark]*

 c) starch *[1 mark]*

2 a) stomata *[1 mark]*

 b) Chloroplast *[1 mark]*. It is the site of photosynthesis *[1 mark]*.

 c) It transports water from the roots to the leaves *[1 mark]*.

 d) phloem *[1 mark]*

 e) i) E.g. they have a large surface area *[1 mark]*.

 ii) E.g. Magnesium for making chlorophyll *[1 mark]* and nitrates for making proteins *[1 mark]*.

3 a) Plants A and D *[1 mark]*.
 They are roughly the same shape and size and so it will be a fair test *[1 mark]*.

 b) Water one of the plants once a week and one twice a week *[1 mark]*. Measure the height of both plants, e.g. once a week, to track the speed of growth of the plants *[1 mark]*.

4 a) The statement given by Anand is his **hypothesis** *[1 mark]*.

 b) Support: E.g. The rate of photosynthesis increases with light intensity between A and C. *[1 mark]*
 Does not support: E.g. The rate of photosynthesis does not increase between C and D. *[1 mark]*

Page 22: Photosynthesis Experiments

1 a) oxygen *[1 mark]*

 b) (Turn measuring cylinder upside down, covering the open end to trap the gas.) Hold a glowing splint inside the measuring cylinder — if it relights, oxygen is present *[1 mark]*.

 c) Any two from: e.g. ensure the plants are the same mass / keep the concentration of the sodium hydrogen carbonate solution the same / keep the light levels the same / make sure all plant samples are healthy / keep the plants in the solution for the same amount of time. *[2 marks — 1 mark for each correct answer]*

2 a) To get rid of all the starch from the plant's leaves *[1 mark]*.

 b) blue-black *[1 mark]*

 c) Boil the leaf in water for a few minutes to soften it *[1 mark]*. Put the leaf in a boiling tube with ethanol and place in hot water to boil the ethanol and remove the chlorophyll from the leaf *[1 mark]*. Dip the leaf in water then drip iodine solution all over the leaf *[1 mark]*. The iodine will not change colour on the part of the leaf that was taped because no starch is present *[1 mark]*.

Page 23: The Importance of Plants

1 algae *[1 mark]*

2 The crop uses energy from sunlight to make glucose during photosynthesis *[1 mark]*. The plants use this glucose to make the organic molecules that become part of their cells *[1 mark]*. This energy is passed on to the chickens when they eat the grain *[1 mark]*.

3 a) Mouse A collapsed because it had used a lot of the oxygen in the jar for respiration *[1 mark]*. In the other jar, the plant took in carbon dioxide and gave out oxygen during photosynthesis *[1 mark]*. This provided a greater supply of oxygen to mouse B, which could therefore respire and survive for longer *[1 mark]*.

 b) It shows that plants are essential in maintaining the levels of oxygen and carbon dioxide in the atmosphere in order for animals to survive *[1 mark]*.

Page 24: Carbon Cycle

1 a) Carbon dioxide is removed from the atmosphere when **plants photosynthesise** *[1 mark]*.

 b) The plants are eaten by the animals *[1 mark]*.

 c) The animals eat other animals *[1 mark]*.

 d) Dead plant and animal remains get buried and form fossil fuels *[1 mark]*.

 e) Decomposers feed on dead plants, animals and animal waste *[1 mark]*. They return carbon dioxide to the atmosphere when they respire *[1 mark]*.

 f) More carbon dioxide is released into the atmosphere than can be removed by plants *[1 mark]*, so the level of carbon dioxide in the atmosphere increases *[1 mark]*.

Page 25: Aerobic Respiration

1 a) Breathing is moving air in and out of the lungs *[1 mark]*, and respiration is a chemical reaction that releases energy from food *[1 mark]*.

b) glucose + oxygen → carbon dioxide + water + energy *[1 mark]*

c) mitochondria *[1 mark]*

d) Glucose comes from eating food, and oxygen is breathed in from the air *[1 mark]*. They are transported in the blood *[1 mark]*.

e) Put limewater in a test tube and use a straw to breathe air into the tube through the solution *[1 mark]*. The limewater will turn cloudy if carbon dioxide is present *[1 mark]*.

f) E.g. building proteins / muscle contraction / keeping warm *[1 mark]*

Page 26: Anaerobic Respiration

1 a) E.g. only aerobic respiration requires oxygen to react with the glucose *[1 mark]*. Aerobic respiration produces carbon dioxide and water *[1 mark]*, whereas anaerobic respiration produces lactic acid *[1 mark]*. Aerobic respiration releases more energy than anaerobic respiration (for every glucose molecule used) *[1 mark]*.

b) glucose → carbon dioxide + ethanol + some energy *[1 mark]*

2 a) Glucose, because yeast needs glucose to respire *[1 mark]*.

b) The number of bubbles produced in boiling tube B *[1 mark]*.

c) Any one from: e.g. count the bubbles produced over a longer time period / contain the bubbles in a measuring cylinder to measure the volume more accurately / repeat their experiment at least three times and calculate the mean *[1 mark]*.

Section B3 — Interactions and Interdependencies

Pages 27-28: Interdependence and Food Webs

1 a) producers *[1 mark]*

b) primary consumer *[1 mark]*

2 a) All the living organisms in an area, plus their habitat *[1 mark]*.

b) seagull *[1 mark]*

c) E.g. a food chain only has one producer, while a food web can have several producers *[1 mark]*.

You would get the mark here for any sensible comparison.

d) plankton → shrimp → herring → seagull, crab → seal

[1 mark for arrow from shrimp to crab, 1 mark for arrows from crab to seagull and seal, 1 mark for arrow from herring to seal.]

3 a) The organisms need each other to survive *[1 mark]*.

b)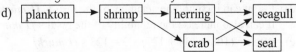

[1 mark]

c) E.g. the number of rabbits would increase because there would be more food available *[1 mark]*.

d) i) E.g. the number of owls might increase because they would be less likely to be eaten by hawks *[1 mark]*.

ii) E.g. the number of frogs might decrease because they are more likely to be eaten, since the number of owls will increase *[1 mark]*.

e) Reason for increase: e.g. the amount of shrubs might increase as there will be no mice to eat them *[1 mark]*. So the number of squirrels might increase because there will be more food available *[1 mark]*.
Reason for decrease: e.g. the number of weasels might decrease as there are no mice for them to eat *[1 mark]*. So the number of squirrels might decrease because they will be more likely to be eaten by foxes (since the foxes will have fewer weasels to eat) *[1 mark]*.

Page 29: Population Size

1 a) Any one from: e.g. food, water, space *[1 mark]*.

b) They kill and eat other organisms *[1 mark]*

c) The antelope population size might decrease because more antelope might be eaten by lions *[1 mark]*.

2 a) quadrat *[1 mark]*

b) $(12 + 8 + 9 + 4 + 7) \div 5 = 40 \div 5 = 8$ *[2 marks for the correct answer, otherwise 1 mark for correct working]*

c) $8 \times 32 = 256$ buttercups *[1 mark]*

Page 30: Protecting Living Things

1 a) The population size of orang-utans could decrease because there would be less food available for them to eat *[1 mark]*, so they might not all be able to survive and reproduce successfully *[1 mark]*

b) Humans use **resources** from the Earth to survive. Human activity has led to **pollution** of the environment and damage to many **habitats**. The human population is **increasing**. So we need to manage the way we use resources to meet our needs without destroying things for future **generations** — this is called **sustainable** development.
[6 marks — 1 mark for each correct word]

2 a) The zoo could breed the oryx in captivity, where they won't be hunted *[1 mark]*. These new oryx could then be released into the wild *[1 mark]*.

b) E.g. protect their habitat from hunters *[1 mark]*.

Section B4 — Genetics and Variation

Pages 31-32: Variation

1 Discontinuous — because there are just four distinct options, not a whole continuous range *[1 mark]*.

2 a) E.g. they can use tools *[1 mark]*. They can walk on two legs *[1 mark]*.

b) i) E.g. gorillas have more hair on their bodies than humans *[1 mark]*. Gorillas have arms that are longer than their legs, whereas human arms are shorter than their legs *[1 mark]*.

ii) They have these differences because their genes are different *[1 mark]*.

3 a) E.g.

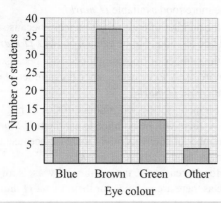

[3 marks — 1 mark for all bars plotted correctly, 1 mark for axes labelled correctly, 1 mark for sensible scale.]

b) E.g. measure the heights up against a wall *[1 mark]* to make sure the ruler/tape measure is vertical *[1 mark]*. Press a flat board onto the student's head *[1 mark]* to flatten down any hair/to make sure the highest point of the body is measured *[1 mark]*.

Any sensible suggestion of how to take accurate measurements with an explanation would be awarded marks for this question.

c) Any three from, e.g. weight / skin colour / intelligence / leaf area *[3 marks — 1 mark for each correct answer]*.

Page 33: Inherited and Environmental Variation

1 a) eye colour *[1 mark]*

b) language *[1 mark]*

2 a) inherited *[1 mark]*

b) i) environmental *[1 mark]*

ii) E.g. Anton could eat more than Marcus *[1 mark]*.

3 a) Any three from: e.g. courgette A could come from a parent plant that grew larger courgettes. / Courgette A could have been grown in better soil conditions. / Courgette A could have got more sunlight than courgette B. / Courgette A could have been grown in a warmer environment than courgette B. / Courgette A could have been watered more than courgette B *[3 marks — 1 mark for each correct answer]*.

b) E.g. because if more than one variable changes in an experiment, it is not a fair test *[1 mark]* so the results won't be valid *[1 mark]*.

Page 34: Classification

1 a) birds *[1 mark]*

b) amphibians *[1 mark]*

2 a) Arthropods have many pairs of jointed legs *[1 mark]*, bodies that are divided into segments *[1 mark]* and hard exoskeletons *[1 mark]*.

b) i) arachnids/spiders *[1 mark]*

ii) It has 8 legs / a 2-part body / no wings/antennae *[1 mark]*.

3 a) Plants are fixed in the ground, whereas animals can move about *[1 mark]*. Plants make their own food, whereas animals cannot do this *[1 mark]*.

b) Fungi can't move around but they also don't make their own food, so they are not the same as plants *[1 mark]*.

c) Protists have a nucleus whereas monerans do not *[1 mark]*.

Page 35: Using Keys

1 A — coleoptera *[1 mark]*
   B — dermaptera *[1 mark]*
   C — megadrilacea *[1 mark]*
   D — spirobolida *[1 mark]*
   E — araneae *[1 mark]*
   F — achatinoidea *[1 mark]*

Section C1 — The Particulate Nature of Matter

Page 36: The Particle Model

1 a) State of matter: liquid *[1 mark]*

Reasoning: because the particles are close but are able to move past one another / are not in a regular arrangement *[1 mark]*.

b) The forces of attraction between solid particles are strong *[1 mark]*, so the particles are held closely together in fixed positions *[1 mark]*. The forces in liquids and gases are weaker *[1 mark]*, so the particles can move past one another/flow to take the shape of the container *[1 mark]*.

2 a) Syringe B, because particles are closer together in liquids than in gases *[1 mark]*, so more particles of liquid can fit into a set volume *[1 mark]*.

b) i) Pull the plunger outwards *[1 mark]*.

ii) No. The forces of attraction between particles stop the liquid from expanding *[1 mark]*.

Pages 37-38: More on The Particle Model

1 a) The air particles bounce off the sides of the mattress at high speeds, creating a pushing force/pressure *[1 mark]*.

b) The pressure increases *[1 mark]*. This is because if there's more air in the mattress, there are more particles bouncing off the sides of the mattress *[1 mark]*.

2 a) The spreading out of the particles of food colouring from a small initial area of high concentration *[1 mark]* to other parts of the water where they are at a lower concentration *[1 mark]*.

b) Brownian motion is the random movement of particles suspended in a liquid/gas *[1 mark]* caused by liquid/gas particles randomly moving about and bumping into the suspended particles *[1 mark]*.

c) i) water temperature *[1 mark]*.

ii) time taken for food colouring to diffuse *[1 mark]*.

iii) volume of food colouring *[1 mark]*.

Remember, the independent variable is the thing you change, the dependent variable is the thing you measure, and the control variables are the things you keep the same.

d) E.g. it can increase the accuracy of the results *[1 mark]*. It can also increase the reliability of the results *[1 mark]*.

e) mean = (108 + 134 + 127) ÷ 3 = 123 s *[1 mark]*

f) E.g. the food colouring diffuses faster in water at 70 °C than in water at 20 °C *[1 mark]*. The diffusion rate is approximately twice as fast at 70 °C than at 20 °C *[1 mark]*.

g) E.g. she could repeat the experiment at other temperatures *[1 mark]*.

This would allow her to see a pattern in her results, e.g. by plotting a temperature-time graph. This wouldn't be valid if she did this with her current method, as there are only two data points/temperatures.

Page 39: Changes of State

1 a) A: melting *[1 mark]*
       B: freezing *[1 mark]*
       C: condensing *[1 mark]*
       D: subliming *[1 mark]*

   b) Evaporation occurs slowly at any temperature *[1 mark]*, whereas boiling occurs rapidly at the boiling point of a substance *[1 mark]*.

2 a) i) The particles move faster *[1 mark]* and move further apart *[1 mark]*.

       ii) The particles move faster because they have more energy at a higher temperature *[1 mark]*. This weakens the forces holding the particles together, which causes them to move further apart *[1 mark]*.

   b) As a result of the particles moving further apart, the ethanol expands as temperature increases *[1 mark]*. This causes the ethanol level to rise up the tube *[1 mark]*.

Page 40: Water

1 a) i) E.g. ice caps / glaciers *[1 mark]*
       ii) water vapour *[1 mark]*

   b) E.g. heat from the Sun makes the water in the ocean evaporate to form water vapour *[1 mark]*. The water vapour rises, cools and condenses to form clouds *[1 mark]*. The water then falls as rain, hail or snow into a lake *[1 mark]*.

   The rain/hail/snow can fall elsewhere on land and be transported to the lake through rivers and glaciers too.

2 a) More evaporation is likely to occur from the dish in the cupboard that has the door open *[1 mark]*.

   b) Measure the volume of water again at the end of the experiment — the difference in volume would be the amount of water that evaporated *[1 mark]*.

   Alternatively, she could weigh each dish at the beginning and end of the experiment, then calculate the difference in mass.

   c) E.g. temperature is a control variable / can affect the rate of evaporation *[1 mark]*, so it needs to be the same in both cupboards *[1 mark]*, otherwise it will be an unfair test / the results will not be valid *[1 mark]*.

Section C2 — Atoms, Elements and Compounds

Page 41: Atoms and Elements

1 a) Different elements contain **different types of atom**. *[1 mark]*

   b) periodic table *[1 mark]*

2 a) C *[1 mark]*
   b) Cl *[1 mark]*
   c) Ca *[1 mark]*
   d) Cu *[1 mark]*
   e) Fe *[1 mark]*

3 a) An atom is a type of tiny particle *[1 mark]*.

   b) An element is a substance that contains only one type of atom *[1 mark]*.

Page 42: Compounds

1 a)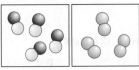

   compound   element   element   mixture

   [4 marks — 1 mark for each correct answer]

   b) Two or more atoms joined together *[1 mark]*.

   c) In an element the molecules are made up of one type of atom joined together *[1 mark]*, whereas in a compound the molecules are made up of different atoms joined together *[1 mark]*.

2 a) hydrogen + oxygen → water *[1 mark]*

   b) A new substance (water) is formed *[1 mark]* which has very different properties from the original elements/ reactants *[1 mark]*.

Page 43: Chemical Formulae

1 a) CO_2 *[1 mark]*
   b) NaOH *[1 mark]*
   c) H_2SO_4 *[1 mark]*

2 A: oxygen *[1 mark]*
   B: water *[1 mark]*
   C: calcium carbonate *[1 mark]*

3 a) sodium chloride *[1 mark]*
   b) copper sulfate *[1 mark]*

4 a) CH_4 *[1 mark]*
   b) methane *[1 mark]*

Pages 44-45: Properties of Metals and Non-Metals

1 a) magnesium oxide *[1 mark]*
   b) 2 *[1 mark]*
   c) zinc *[1 mark]*

2 a) non-metal *[1 mark]*
   b) malleability *[1 mark]*
   c) Most non-metals are electrical insulators *[1 mark]* because the atoms are arranged so that charged particles (electrons) can't move through them *[1 mark]*.

3 a) Samples 1 and 3 *[1 mark]*
   b) Sample 2 *[1 mark]*
   c) An electrical conductor *[1 mark]* because metals contain some charged particles (electrons) that are free to move between the atoms and carry electric current *[1 mark]*.

4 a) Metals are thermal conductors *[1 mark]*. This means they let heat energy pass through so it can be transferred to the food in the saucepan *[1 mark]*.

   b) E.g. non-metals are thermal insulators *[1 mark]*. This means not much heat is transferred from the pan through the handle *[1 mark]*, so the handle doesn't get too hot to hold *[1 mark]*.

Section C3 — Pure and Impure Substances

Pages 46-47: Purity and Mixtures

1 a) A pure substance is always made up of **particles of only one element or one compound** *[1 mark]*.
   b) The citric acid wasn't pure *[1 mark]*.

2 a) water *[1 mark]*
   b) sugar *[1 mark]*
   c) 25 g + 100 g = 125 g *[1 mark]*
   Remember, mass is conserved when solids are dissolved, so: mass of solution = mass of solute + mass of solvent
   d) The forces holding the sugar molecules together break *[1 mark]*. The sugar molecules mix with the water molecules to form a solution *[1 mark]*. The sugar molecules are distributed randomly throughout the water *[1 mark]*.

3 a) A mixture is a substance made up of two or more different substances which aren't chemically joined *[1 mark]*.
   b) i) oxygen *[1 mark]*
      ii) nitrogen *[1 mark]*
      iii) E.g. argon / carbon dioxide / water vapour *[1 mark]*.
      iv) oxygen *[1 mark]*

4 a) physical change *[1 mark]*
   b) The dish would contain white crystals / salt crystals *[1 mark]*. Over the week, the water would evaporate *[1 mark]*, leaving the solid salt behind *[1 mark]*.

Page 48: Solvents and Solutions

1 water *[1 mark]*
2 a) A solution in which no more solute will dissolve *[1 mark]*.
   b) i) The solvent used *[1 mark]*.
      ii) The mass of sodium bromide that dissolved in each solvent *[1 mark]*.
   c) Water *[1 mark]*, because the largest mass of sodium bromide dissolved in the water *[1 mark]*.
   d) More sodium bromide, because solubility increases with temperature *[1 mark]*.

Page 49: More on Water

1 a) To make her experiment a fair test. / The volume of water is a control variable *[1 mark]*.
   b)

Dish	Type of water	Mass of solid left in dish (g)
1	**seawater**	1.06
2	**tap water**	0.03
3	**distilled water**	0.00

[2 marks for all three correct, or 1 mark for one correct.]

   c) E.g. heat the sample of the water until it boils and record its boiling point *[1 mark]*. If the water is pure, it will boil at the same temperature as pure water / 100 °C *[1 mark]*.

2 When most substances freeze, their particles get closer together. This makes the substances **more** dense. When water freezes, the particles get further apart. So ice is **less** dense than liquid water. This means that when you freeze water it **increases** in volume. *[1 mark for each correct answer]*

Pages 50-52: Separating Mixtures

1 a) suspension *[1 mark]*
   b)

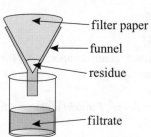

filter paper
funnel
residue
filtrate

[3 marks for all four labels correct, 2 marks for any two labels correct, or 1 mark for any 1 label correct]

2 a) The blue dye *[1 mark]*, because it has moved out the furthest from the centre of the paper *[1 mark]*.
   b) Any one from: e.g. the solvent (the water) / the type of filter paper / the distance between the top of the water and the food colouring / the amount of food colouring / the length of time that the wick is kept in the water for *[1 mark]*.

3 a) distillation *[1 mark]*
   b) E.g. the inside of the Liebig condenser tube is cold *[1 mark]*. When the hot gas leaving the flask enters the condenser, it cools and condenses back into liquid water *[1 mark]*.
   c) When you turn off the heat, the air in the flask cools and contracts, which could suck liquid back into the flask *[1 mark]*.
   d) The colour of the squash would get darker *[1 mark]* because as the water evaporates, the solution in the flask will become more concentrated *[1 mark]*.

4 a) three *[1 mark]*
   b) Pen B *[1 mark]* because it has the same number of spots in the same positions as the sample *[1 mark]*.

5 How to mark your answer:

0 marks:	There is no relevant information.
1-2 marks:	A simple method is given, but some main points are missing. The points made are not linked together.
3-4 marks:	An experimental method is outlined in detail. Most of the main points are included. Some of the points made are linked together.
5-6 marks:	All of the main points and at least one of the extra points are covered. The points made are well-linked and the answer has a clear and logical structure.

Here are some points your answer may include:

Main Points
Grind up the rock salt using a pestle and mortar.
Add the ground up mixture to water and stir well.
Line a funnel with a piece of filter paper.
Pour the mixture into the funnel.
The salt solution will pass through the filter paper, but the rock and sand will be left behind.
Place the salt solution in an evaporating dish.
Heat gently with a Bunsen burner / leave the dish in a warm place until all the water has evaporated.
Pure salt crystals will be left in the dish.

Answers

Extra points

When you add water to the ground up mixture, the salt will dissolve, but the rock and sand will stay as solids (because they're insoluble).

The solid particles of rock and sand won't fit through the tiny holes in the filter paper, so they collect on the paper.

The dissolved salt particles are small enough to fit through the holes in the filter paper, so they pass through the paper into the beaker (along with the water).

Section C4 — Chemical Reactions

Pages 53-54: Everyday Chemical Reactions

1 a) The air hole should be half-open *[1 mark]*.
   b) Closing the air hole of the Bunsen burner **decreases the temperature of the flame because it decreases the amount of air entering the burner** *[1 mark]*.
   c) i) yellow/orange *[1 mark]*
       ii) Any two from: e.g. put a heat-resistant mat under the burner / tie long hair back / don't wear loose clothing / handle any objects that have been heated with tongs/gloves *[1 mark each for any sensible safety precautions, up to a maximum of 2 marks.]*
   d) E.g.

   [1 mark for a circle drawn around the top of the inner cone.]

2 a) ice melting *[1 mark]*
   b) Any one from: e.g. zinc oxide / magnesium oxide *[1 mark]*.

3 a) The bananas in the sealed container will ripen faster than the bananas on the counter *[1 mark]*.
   b) Any one from: e.g. the number of bananas in the bunch / the size of the bananas / the variety of the bananas / the ripeness of the bananas / the length of time the bananas were left for *[1 mark]*.
   c) So that the experiment is a fair test *[1 mark]*.
   d) The bananas kept in the container have more brown spots, so they have ripened more *[1 mark]*. So keeping bananas in a sealed container causes them to ripen faster *[1 mark]*.

Page 55: More on Chemical Reactions

1 a) Because the powder has visibly changed colour / because the powder has turned from white to yellow *[1 mark]*.
   b) Difference in mass = mass before – mass after
                        = 40.0 – 39.3 = 0.7 g *[1 mark]*
   c) Some mass may have escaped in the form of gas during the reaction *[1 mark]*.
   d) Because the total number of each type of atom is the same before and after the reaction *[1 mark]*.
   e) E.g. repeat the experiment and calculate the mean difference in mass *[1 mark]*.

Pages 56-57: Combustion and Oxidation

1 a) Combustion is when a substance **burns** in oxygen to release energy. An example of a combustion reaction is **a bonfire**. *[2 marks — 1 mark for each correct answer.]*
   b) Because the substance reacts and combines with oxygen *[1 mark]*.

2 The limewater will turn cloudy *[1 mark]*.

3 a) iron oxide / rust *[1 mark]*
   b) rusting / oxidation *[1 mark]*

4 a) fuel / unburnt wood *[1 mark]*
   b) If the glowing splint is held in oxygen, it will relight *[1 mark]*.

5 a) The iron reacts with the oxygen in the air to make iron oxide, which removes the oxygen from the air *[1 mark]*. The water rises to fill the space the oxygen took up *[1 mark]*.
   b) The volume of air in the test tube has decreased by 20 – 16 = 4 cm³ *[1 mark]*
       So the amount of air in the tube has decreased by (4 ÷ 20) × 100 = 20% *[1 mark]*
       This is the amount of gas in the air that was able to react with the iron *[1 mark]*. The gas reacting with the iron is oxygen, so it can be concluded that 20% of the air in the test tube is oxygen *[1 mark]*.

Page 58: Thermal Decomposition Reactions

1 a) blue *[1 mark]*
   b) It would change from white to blue *[1 mark]*.

2 a) copper oxide *[1 mark]*
   b) carbon dioxide *[1 mark]*
   c) copper carbonate → copper oxide + carbon dioxide *[1 mark]*

3 a) It changes from purple *[1 mark]* to green *[1 mark]*.
   b) potassium manganate *[1 mark]*, manganese dioxide *[1 mark]*, oxygen *[1 mark]*

Pages 59-60: Reactivity Series and Metal Extraction

1 a) Gold is found in the ground **on its own** but sodium is found **combined with other substances**. This is because gold is **not very reactive** and sodium is **very reactive**. *[4 marks — 1 mark for each correct answer.]*
   b) E.g. jewellery / electrical contacts *[1 mark]*
   c) E.g. roofing/piping for houses *[1 mark]* because lead is not very reactive *[1 mark]*, so it won't corrode when it comes into contact with water/air *[1 mark]*.

2 a) From most to least reactive: potassium, **sodium**, **magnesium**, carbon, **copper**, silver *[2 marks for all three correct, otherwise 1 mark for one correct.]*
   b) carbon *[1 mark]*

3 a) The iron has reacted with oxygen and water in the air / with water on the ground *[1 mark]*.
   b) The oil creates a barrier between the iron chain and oxygen and water *[1 mark]* but still allows the chain to move *[1 mark]*.
   c) E.g. painting / coating with plastic *[1 mark]*

4 a)

Metal	Extracted using carbon?	
	Yes	No
zinc	✓	
potassium		✓
lead	✓	
calcium		✓
magnesium		✓

[5 marks — 1 mark for each correct row.]

b) iron oxide + carbon → iron + carbon dioxide *[1 mark]*

c) Aluminium is higher than carbon in the reactivity series / is more reactive than carbon *[1 mark]*.

Page 61: Reactions of Metals with Oxygen and Water

1 a) A, C, B *[1 mark]*

b) hydrogen *[1 mark]*

c) E.g. metal A will react the most vigorously with oxygen and metal B will react the least vigorously *[1 mark]*.

2 a) oxidation *[1 mark]*

b) Most metals react with oxygen to form a metal **oxide.** *[1 mark]*

c) Calcium *[1 mark]* because it is the most reactive / highest in the reactivity series *[1 mark]*.

Page 62: Displacement Reactions

1 a) The aluminium displaces the iron metal from the iron oxide *[1 mark]* because it is more reactive than iron *[1 mark]*.

b) aluminium oxide *[1 mark]*

2 a) Any two from: e.g. the volume of zinc sulfate in each test tube / the size/shape of the metal strips / the amount of time the metal strips spent in the solution. *[2 marks — 1 mark for each correct answer]*

b) magnesium sulfate + zinc *[1 mark]*

c) magnesium, zinc, metal X, copper *[1 mark]*

Page 63: Acids and Alkalis

1 a) drain cleaner *[1 mark]*

b) E.g. pH 2 (accept any value between 0 and 3) *[1 mark]*

c) E.g. she could add a drop of vinegar to blue litmus paper *[1 mark]*. Acidic solutions will turn blue litmus paper red *[1 mark]*.

2 a) (7.2 + 7.8 + 7.0 + 7.7 + 8.0 + 8.5) ÷ 6 = 46.2 ÷ 6 = 7.7 *[1 mark]*

b) E.g. so that the results are more likely to represent the whole garden (rather than only represent one area) *[1 mark]*.

c) E.g. repeat the tests at more sample sites and average the results *[1 mark]*.

d) They won't grow well, because the soil is slightly alkaline / the pH is too high *[1 mark]*.

Pages 64-65: Neutralisation

1 a) copper sulfate — sulfuric acid *[1 mark]*
sodium nitrate — nitric acid *[1 mark]*
zinc chloride — hydrochloric acid *[1 mark]*

b) water *[1 mark]*

2 a) E.g. Universal indicator *[1 mark]*

b) sodium chloride *[1 mark]*

c) E.g. wear eye protection / safety goggles / gloves when handling the solutions *[1 mark]*.

d) His final pH reading is lower than 7 / is acidic *[1 mark]*. This shows he has added too much acid *[1 mark]* so there is leftover/unreacted acid in the solution as well as the salt *[1 mark]*.

3 a) water *[1 mark]* + carbon dioxide *[1 mark]*

b) calcium sulfate *[1 mark]*

c) A substance that will react with an acid to form a salt and water *[1 mark]*.

4 a) potassium chloride *[1 mark]*

b) E.g. pour the salt solution into the evaporating dish and heat it using the Bunsen burner *[1 mark]*. Heat the solution until about a third of the original amount of the solution is left in the dish *[1 mark]*. Leave the solution so that the rest of the water can evaporate *[1 mark]*.

Pages 66-67: Reactions of Metals with Acids

1 a)

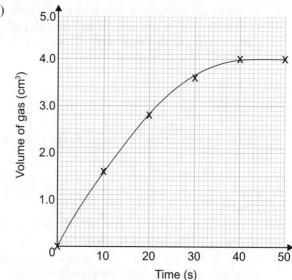

[1 mark for correctly plotted points, 1 mark for curved line of best fit]

b) i) hydrogen *[1 mark]*
ii) There should be a squeaky pop *[1 mark]*.

c) aluminium chloride *[1 mark]*

d) E.g. for each metal, measure the volume of gas produced in a fixed time *[1 mark]*. The more gas there is, the more reactive the metal is *[1 mark]*.
Alternatively, you could have said to measure the time taken to produce a fixed volume of gas for each metal — the less time taken, the more reactive the metal.

2 a) Any two from: e.g. an equal amount of acid was used in each test tube. / An equal amount of metal was used in each test tube. / The test tubes were kept at the same temperature. *[2 marks — 1 mark for each correct answer]*

b) D *[1 mark]* — copper is less reactive than hydrogen so will not react *[1 mark]*.

c) B *[1 mark]* — magnesium is the most reactive of the three metals, so will react the most vigorously with the acid *[1 mark]*.

Page 68: Limestone

1 a) calcium carbonate *[1 mark]*
  b) i) It can be damaged by acid rain *[1 mark]*.
    ii) Any two from: e.g. making cement / making mortar / making concrete / making glass *[2 marks — 1 mark for each correct answer]*
  c) calcium oxide *[1 mark]*
2 a) i) It increases soil pH *[1 mark]*.
    ii) neutralisation reaction *[1 mark]*
  b) Limestone is heated to produce calcium oxide (and carbon dioxide) *[1 mark]*. Water is then added to the calcium oxide to make agricultural lime *[1 mark]*.

Page 69: Acids and the Environment

1 a) carbon dioxide *[1 mark]*
  b) e.g. sulfur dioxide *[1 mark]*
  c) Statue B *[1 mark]* because copper is less reactive than hydrogen / lower down the reactivity series, so it should not react with the acids in acid rain *[1 mark]*. Iron and magnesium are more reactive than hydrogen / higher up the reactivity series, so they will react with the acids and corrode *[1 mark]*. Limestone contains calcium carbonate, which will react with the acids and so damage the statue *[1 mark]*.
2 a) chemical weathering *[1 mark]*
  b) E.g. large cities produce more of the gases that form acid rain / large cities produce more pollution *[1 mark]*.

Page 70: The Effects of Fossil Fuels

1 a) oxygen *[1 mark]*
  b) solid particles/particulates of carbon/soot/unburnt fuel *[1 mark]*, carbon monoxide *[1 mark]*
2 a) E.g. there was an increase in the amount of carbon dioxide in the atmosphere between 1850 and 2000 *[1 mark]*.
  b) E.g. because carbon dioxide traps heat from the Sun in the Earth's atmosphere *[1 mark]* so more carbon dioxide could trap more heat (so the atmosphere would get warmer) *[1 mark]*.
  c) Any one from: e.g. reduce the amount of fossil fuels we burn / reduce deforestation / plant more trees *[1 mark]*.

Section P1 — Energy

Page 71: Energy Transfer

1 a) chemical *[1 mark]*
  b) elastic *[1 mark]*
  c) electrical *[1 mark]*
2 a) Elastic (strain) energy *[1 mark]* to kinetic energy *[1 mark]*.
  b) Chemical energy *[1 mark]* to thermal and light energy *[1 mark]*.
  c) Electrical energy *[1 mark]* to sound energy *[1 mark]*.
3 a) gravitational potential energy *[1 mark]*
  b) i) Gravitational potential energy to kinetic energy *[1 mark]*.
    ii) Kinetic energy to sound energy *[1 mark]*.

Page 72: Conservation of Energy

1 24 000 J *[1 mark]*
  The total input is equal to the total output, which is 15 600 + 4800 + 3600 = 24 000 J.
2 Energy can never be created or destroyed — it's only ever transferred from one form to another *[1 mark]*.
3 a) the wasted energy = total energy input – the useful energy
    = 12 – 3
    = 9 J *[1 mark]*
  b) The bulb usefully transfers electrical energy to light energy *[1 mark]*. Energy is always wasted when usefully transferring energy, and this wasted energy is transferred to thermal energy by the bulb *[1 mark]*.
  c) Energy can't be created, it can only be transferred from one form to another *[1 mark]*.
  She's actually transferring kinetic energy to thermal energy.

Pages 73-74: Energy Resources

1 a) plants *[1 mark]*
  b) heats atmosphere *[1 mark]*
2 The Sun warms up water in seas, lakes and rivers, causing it to **evaporate** and turn into water vapour. As the water vapour rises it **cools down**, causing it to **condense** into lots of tiny droplets of liquid water — otherwise known as clouds. The water can then fall to the ground again as rain, **snow/hail** or **hail/snow**. *[5 marks — 1 mark for each correct answer]*
3 a) chemical energy *[1 mark]*
  b) By connecting the battery to an electrical circuit *[1 mark]*.
4 a) E.g. wood *[1 mark]*
  b) E.g. wind power *[1 mark]* and wave power *[1 mark]*.
5 a) Coal *[1 mark]*, oil *[1 mark]* and gas *[1 mark]*.
  b) Light energy from the Sun is absorbed by plants during photosynthesis *[1 mark]*. Creatures can absorb this energy by eating the plants *[1 mark]*. Some of this energy is stored in the tissues of both the plants and animals *[1 mark]*. When plants and animals die they can become buried and slowly decay, and over millions of years the pressure turns these remains into fossil fuels *[1 mark]*.
  c) By burning them *[1 mark]*.
6 a) The Sun heats up some parts of the Earth's surface more than others *[1 mark]*. Above the warmer bits of land (or sea) you get pockets of warm air *[1 mark]*. This warm air rises and cold air rushes in to fill its place, causing a wind to blow *[1 mark]*.
  b) wave power *[1 mark]*

Page 75: Generating Electricity

1 solar power *[1 mark]*
2 Electricity is generated from wave power by **waves pushing air in and out of a turbine**. *[1 mark]*
3 a) Coal is burnt in a boiler, which releases heat energy *[1 mark]*. This is used to heat up water which then changes to high pressure steam *[1 mark]*. The steam is then used to drive a turbine *[1 mark]*. The turbine is attached to a generator, which spins and transfers kinetic energy into electrical energy *[1 mark]*.

b) The wind turns the blades of the wind turbine, which turns the generator inside *[1 mark]*. The generator transfers kinetic energy into electrical energy *[1 mark]*.

c) Location A — the top of a hill is more exposed and therefore likely to be windier, so the turbines could generate more electricity *[1 mark]*.

Page 76: Renewable and Non-Renewable Energy Resources

1 a) Non-renewable energy resources can't be replaced in a person's lifetime, whereas renewable energy resources can be replaced in a person's lifetime *[1 mark]*.

b) Any two from: e.g. coal/oil/gas/nuclear fuel. *[2 marks — 1 mark for each correct answer]*

c) Any three from: e.g. biomass/wind/wave/solar/ hydroelectric. *[3 marks — 1 mark for each correct answer]*

2 How to grade your answer:

0 marks:	There is no relevant information.
1-2 marks:	At least one correct advantage or disadvantage has been given. The answer is not very clear and has no structure.
3-4 marks:	There is a description of advantages and disadvantages. Most of the main points have been covered. The answer has some detail and structure.
5-6 marks:	There is a detailed discussion of the advantages and disadvantages. Most of the main points and at least one of the extra points have been covered. The answer is clear and has a logical structure.

Here are some points your answer may include:

<u>Main points</u>
Solar power is a renewable resource and so won't run out, but coal could run out as it is non-renewable.
If more solar power is used, less coal will be used, which means the coal won't run out as quickly.
Using more solar power and less coal will reduce the overall amount of pollutants released whilst electricity is being generated.
It would cost a lot of money for the government to build the solar panels.
Solar panels don't produce as much energy as a coal-fired power station, so the government would need to build a lot of solar panels to get a substantial amount of energy.
Solar panels depend on the amount of sunlight, so are not as reliable as coal.

<u>Extra points</u>
Light from the Sun is free, but coal costs money, so it will be cheaper for the country once the solar panels are up and running.
Although burning coal damages the environment, the initial set-up of the solar panels would also cause some damage to the environment, whereas the coal-fired power station already exists.
Carbon dioxide and sulfur dioxide released from burning coal can lead to global warming and acid rain.

Section P2 — Motion and Forces

Page 77: Speed

1 speed = distance ÷ time
     = 6600 ÷ 12
     = 550 mph *[1 mark]*

2 a) speed = distance ÷ time
     = 900 ÷ 1000
     = 0.9 m/s *[1 mark]*

b) speed = distance ÷ time $\Rightarrow$ time = distance ÷ speed
time = 10 ÷ 40 = 0.25 hours *[2 marks for the correct answer, otherwise 1 mark for correct substitution.]*

3 a) Record the time taken for each horse to run the length of the track *[1 mark]*. Divide the length of the track by each time taken to get the average speed of each horse *[1 mark]*.

b) Repeat the test multiple times and take an average of the result for each horse *[1 mark]*.

c) E.g. She should allow recovery time between each repeat / the weather conditions should be similar for both horses/for all repeats *[1 mark]*.

Page 78: More on Speed

1 Relative speed = speed of car + speed of bus
     = 73 + 56 = 129 mph
[2 marks for correct answer, otherwise 1 mark for knowing that relative speed = speed of car + speed of bus.]

2 a) It is moving at a steady speed *[1 mark]* towards the ground *[1 mark]*.

b) speed = gradient = change in y ÷ change in x
     = (4 – 1) ÷ (2.5 – 1.0) = 3 ÷ 1.5 = 2 m/s
[2 marks for correct answer, otherwise 1 mark for dividing the change in distance by the change in time.]

c) 4.75 s *[1 mark for any time between 4.6 s and 4.9 s.]*

Page 79: Forces

1 a) It is a push or a pull that occurs when two objects interact *[1 mark]*.

b) i) newtons *[1 mark]*
   ii) newton meter / force meter *[1 mark]*

c) Any two from: E.g. Slow down *[1 mark]* / stop moving *[1 mark]* / change direction *[1 mark]* / turn *[1 mark]* / change shape *[1 mark]*

2 It will slow down the car *[1 mark]*.

3

[1 mark for drawing an arrow of equal length, 1 mark for drawing the arrow pointing backwards.]

Pages 80-81: Springs

1 a) The extension of a spring is directly proportional to the force applied to it *[1 mark]*.

b) Force = spring constant × extension
     = 60 × 0.1 = 6 N *[1 mark]*

2 a) downwards *[1 mark]*

b) 20 cm = 0.2 m
Force = spring constant × extension
= 25 × 0.2 = 5 N *[1 mark]*

3 For one spring:
force = spring constant × extension
⇒ extension = force ÷ spring constant
= 9.0 ÷ 60 = 0.15 m

For springs in parallel,
total extension = extension of one spring ÷ number of springs.
So the extension of the two springs in parallel is
0.15 ÷ 2 = 0.075 m
[2 marks for the correct answer, otherwise 1 mark for knowing that the extension will be half that of one spring.]

4 a) i) The weight hung on the spring *[1 mark]*.
       ii) The extension of the spring *[1 mark]*.

   b)

Weight (N)	Extension (cm)			
	Reading One	Reading Two	Reading Three	Mean
0.1	0.9	1.0	0.8	0.9
0.2	1.9	1.9	1.9	1.9
0.3	2.7	2.3	2.5	2.5
0.4	3.6	3.9	3.6	**3.7**
0.5	4.5	4.6	4.4	**4.5**

[2 marks available — 1 mark for each correct answer.]

   c) i)

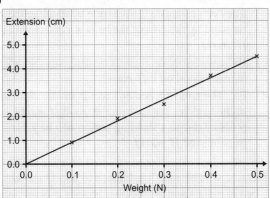

[3 marks available — 1 mark for drawing graph to a sensible scale, 1 mark for plotting points correctly, 1 mark for drawing suitable line of best fit.]
       ii) 0.39 N *[1 mark for a weight between 0.38 N and 0.40 N.]*

Pages 82-83: Balanced and Unbalanced Forces

1 a) speeding up *[1 mark]*
   b) accelerating upwards *[1 mark]*

2 a) Overall force = 130 000 – 50 000 = 80 000 N *[1 mark]*
   b) The forces acting on the train are balanced / the force provided by the train's engine is equal and opposite to the resistive forces acting on the train *[1 mark]*.

3 a) The spring and the weight are in **equilibrium** and the forces on each object are **balanced** *[1 mark]*.
   b) Overall force = 5.5 – 3.0 = 2.5 N *[1 mark]*

4 a) The cherry will stay on top of the frosting *[1 mark]*.
   b) The cherry will sink into the frosting *[1 mark]*.

5 a) Overall horizontal force = 6000 – (7000 + 1000)
= –2000 N

The forces are unbalanced because there is an overall backwards force of 2000 N *[1 mark]*.
   b) The car moves at a constant speed *[1 mark]*.

Pages 84-85: Friction and Resistance

1 a) Friction is a force between two surfaces that always acts in the opposite direction to movement *[1 mark]*.
   b) i) E.g. It allows the skater to grip the ice to steer and control his/her movement *[1 mark]* / it allows the skater to stop *[1 mark]*.
       ii) E.g. It wastes the skater's energy *[1 mark]* / it limits the skater's top speed *[1 mark]*.

2 a) The resistive forces acting on him will be reduced *[1 mark]*.
This will cause his falling speed to increase *[1 mark]*.
   b) The air resistance on the skydiver increases with their speed *[1 mark]*.
   c) Air resistance and weight become equal/balanced, so no overall force is acting on the skydiver *[1 mark]*.

3 a) How to grade your answer:
0 marks: There is no relevant information.
1-2 marks: A simple method to measure the effects of parachute surface area on drag is partly outlined. Includes some main points but omits key details. The points made are not linked together.
3-4 marks: A method to measure the effects of parachute surface area on drag is outlined in some detail. Includes most of the main points and one extra point. Some of the points made are linked together.
5-6 marks: A method to measure the effects of parachute surface area on drag is fully explained in detail. Includes all of the main points and at least two extra points. The points made are well-linked and the answer has a clear and logical structure.
Here are some points your answer may include:
Main points
Cut different sizes of square parachutes out of the plastic.
Record the area of the parachutes by measuring the side length and squaring it.
Mark the point above the ground that the weight will be dropped from.
Hold the parachute and weight at the fixed height.
Get someone to start a stopwatch when the weight is released and stop it when the weight touches the ground.
Record the time taken for the weight to hit the ground.
The longer the weight takes to touch the ground, the lower its average speed and so the greater the drag of the parachute.
Repeat the procedure for each area of parachute.

Extra points

Keep all factors except for the parachute size the same, e.g. the weight, the method of attachment, the shape of the parachute, the plastic the parachute is made from. Repeat for each area and take the mean of the time. Measurements should be taken inside or in clear weather if outside to reduce the effect of wind on the outcome. Hold each parachute open before it is dropped to make sure every parachute is open from the start. Use a large height e.g. a window or a balcony to get better results.

b) To make sure her results are reliable *[1 mark]*.

c) E.g. To help the parachute keep its shape *[1 mark]* / to stop the parachute from being blown off course *[1 mark]*.

d) Increasing the area of the parachute makes it less streamlined *[1 mark]*, so the bigger the area of the parachute, the larger the drag it provides and the slower it will fall *[1 mark]*.

Page 86: Stopping Distances

1 a) Any two from: e.g. the speed of the car *[1 mark]* / tiredness of the driver *[1 mark]* / whether the driver is under the influence of alcohol/drugs *[1 mark]* / attitude of the driver *[1 mark]* / the car's brakes *[1 mark]* / the car's tyres *[1 mark]* / road surface *[1 mark]* / weather conditions *[1 mark]*.

b) Car A, because it is travelling at a higher speed *[1 mark]*.

2 a) i) Stopping distance decreases with speed *[1 mark]*, so at 20 mph the stopping distance of a car is relatively low, meaning they can stop quickly when they see a hazard and are more likely to avoid a collision *[1 mark]*.

ii) There are likely to be more hazards around schools, such as children in the road *[1 mark]*.

b) Ice on the road can cause cars to skid when braking, increasing stopping distance *[1 mark]*. Spreading salt to melt the ice stops cars from skidding and reduces the stopping distances of the cars *[1 mark]*.

Page 87: Forces and Rotation

1 D *[1 mark]*

2 Wheelbarrow B, since it has a longer handle *[1 mark]*. This acts as a longer lever, so the turning force about the wheel is greater for a given effort force, making the load easier to lift *[1 mark]*.

3 a) A lever is a machine that makes doing work easier by multiplying the force you put in *[1 mark]*.

b) The further away the effort is applied from the hinge, the greater the turning force about the hinge for a given effort force, so the easier it is to move the door *[1 mark]*.

Page 88: Moments

1 a) moment = force × perpendicular distance
clockwise moment = 12 × 3 = 36 Ncm *[1 mark]*
anticlockwise moment = 8 × 5 = 40 Ncm *[1 mark]*
The anticlockwise moment about the pivot is greater, so the ruler will rotate anticlockwise *[1 mark]*.

b) anticlockwise moment = 8 × 3 = 24 Ncm *[1 mark]*
So clockwise moment = 12 × perpendicular distance = 24 Ncm
⇒ perpendicular distance = 24 ÷ 12 = 2 cm *[1 mark]*
The force needs to be 2 cm from the pivot, so it should be applied at 7 cm on the ruler *[1 mark]*.

2 a) distance from pivot to applied force = 15 − 2
= 13 cm
clockwise moment = force × perpendicular distance
= 22 × 13 = 286 Ncm
[2 marks for correct answer, otherwise 1 mark for calculating the distance from the pivot to the applied force.]

b) distance from pivot to force exerted = 2 cm
moment = force × perpendicular distance
⇒ force = moment ÷ perpendicular distance
The moments are the same on both sides, so
force = 286 ÷ 2 = 143 N
[2 marks for correct answer, otherwise 1 mark for knowing the moments are the same on both sides.]

Pages 89-90: Pressure

1 Pressure is calculated using the force applied at an angle of **90°** to an area. The greater the area over which the force acts, the **smaller** the pressure. *[1 mark]*

2 a) pressure = force ÷ area = 0.20 ÷ 2.5 = 0.08 N/cm² *[1 mark]*

b) pressure = force ÷ area
⇒ area = force ÷ pressure = 0.20 ÷ 0.4 = 0.5 cm²
[2 marks for correct answer, otherwise 1 mark for correct substitution.]

3 Snowshoes increase the area over which the force of a person's weight is applied *[1 mark]*. Pressure = force ÷ area, so the pressure on the ground due to the person's weight decreases *[1 mark]*, so the person will not sink into the snow as much when walking *[1 mark]*.

4 a) The thickness of the wood *[1 mark]*.

b) They can calculate the pressure by dividing the weight of the sand by the area of the bags in contact with the wood *[1 mark]*.

c) If the wood breaks it could be dangerous/unsafe for humans stood on it *[1 mark]*.

d) E.g. The area of a person's feet is smaller than the area of the bags in contact with the wood *[1 mark]*, so the pressure due to a standing person will be greater than the bags of sand *[1 mark]*.

5 An individual nail point has a small area and so a large pressure which causes the balloon to pop *[1 mark]*. For a bed of nails, the nails together provide a larger area to distribute the weight of the balloon *[1 mark]*. This means the pressure on the balloon from each nail is much lower than when using one nail, so the nails don't pop the balloon *[1 mark]*.

Pages 91-92: Density

1 a) density = mass ÷ volume *[1 mark]*

b) i) Volume = length × width × height
= 1.2 × 0.6 × 2.0 = 1.44 cm³ *[1 mark]*

ii) density = mass ÷ volume ⇒ mass = density × volume
mass = 2.5 × 1.44 = 3.6 g
[2 marks for correct answer, otherwise 1 mark for correct substitution.]

c) The actual mass of the pendant will be lower because the estimated volume is larger than the actual volume of the pendant *[1 mark]*.

The estimated volume didn't account for the rounded corners that don't fill the volume of a cuboid.

d) E.g. Pour water from the jug into the measuring cylinder so that it is partly filled, and measure the volume of the water *[1 mark]*. Drop the pendant into the water so that it is submerged, and measure the new level of the water *[1 mark]*. The volume of the pendant is equal to the change in level of the water *[1 mark]*.

2   He should measure the mass of an empty beaker, then pour the liquid in and measure the mass of the beaker and liquid. The change in mass is equal to the mass of the liquid *[1 mark]*. He should find the volume of the liquid by reading off the scale *[1 mark]*. He can then calculate the density using density = mass ÷ volume *[1 mark]*.

3   a) volume of spoon
= volume of water and spoon – volume of water
= 255.0 – 250.0 = 5.0 cm³ *[1 mark]*
b) Density = mass ÷ volume = 45 ÷ 5.0
= 9.0 g/cm³ *[1 mark]*

The density of the spoon is closest to the density of the copper, so the spoon is most likely to be made from copper *[1 mark]*.

You'll still get the mark for part b) if the answer you used from part a) was wrong.

Section P3 — Waves

Page 93: Sound

1   a) E.g. when the air was removed, there was a vacuum inside the jar *[1 mark]*. Sound can't travel in a vacuum as there are no particles to pass on the sound wave vibrations *[1 mark]*.
b) Sound can travel through solids, so the ringing is able to pass through the base of the jar *[1 mark]*. The foam beneath the clock absorbed this sound *[1 mark]*.

2   a) E.g. Sound travels faster through solids than gases *[1 mark]*, so the sound waves travelled faster through the ground and reached Russell sooner than the sound waves travelling through the air *[1 mark]*.
b) E.g. the sound waves were reflected off the cliff and back towards Russell *[1 mark]*. This means these sound waves had to travel further, so the sound reached him later *[1 mark]*.

Page 94: More on Sound

1   a) i) The number of complete waves that pass a point in one second *[1 mark]*.
ii) The higher the frequency of a noise, the higher pitched it is *[1 mark]*.

If you write this the other way round (the lower the frequency, the lower the pitch) that's fine.

b) i) road drill *[1 mark]*
ii) scream *[1 mark]*

The scream has the greatest amplitude, so it is the loudest sound.

2   a) When sound waves hit the diaphragm in a microphone, the diaphragm vibrates back and forth *[1 mark]*. The microphone changes these vibrations into electrical signals *[1 mark]*.
b) e.g. a loud speaker *[1 mark]*

Page 95: Hearing

1   a) The vibrations in the sound wave cause the eardrum to vibrate *[1 mark]*. The vibrations are passed along the solid ear bones to the cochlea *[1 mark]*.
b) To prevent damage to their hearing *[1 mark]*.

2   a) E.g. Matthew could start by playing sounds with frequencies much higher than 20 000 Hz *[1 mark]*. Then he could play sounds of gradually decreasing frequency until the person raises their hand *[1 mark]*.

The typical auditory range of humans is 20 to 20 000 Hz, but some people might be able to hear sounds higher than 20 000 Hz — that's why Matthew should make sure the starting frequency is above this.

b) Any two from: e.g. the loudspeaker should be set at the same volume *[1 mark]*. / They should be sat at the same distance from the loudspeaker *[1 mark]*. / The increases or decreases in frequency should be the same size *[1 mark]*. / They should have the same number of attempts at hearing a frequency *[1 mark]*.

Pages 96-97: Light

1   a) The pinhole needs to be small so that **only one ray from each point on the object gets into the camera.** *[1 mark]*
b) i) E.g.

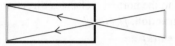

[1 mark for drawing two lines from the object through the pinhole to the paper, 1 mark for drawing arrows pointing in the correct direction.]

ii) The image will be upside down and crossed over/ flipped because the rays of light cross over as they pass through the pinhole *[1 mark]*.

2   a) Luminous object *[1 mark]*
b) Light travels at a finite speed *[1 mark]*. Stars are a long distance away from the Earth, so it takes time for their light to travel through space to the Earth *[1 mark]*.

3   a) Light travels so fast that the light will reach the sensor almost instantly *[1 mark]*. The sensor can only measure to the nearest hundredth of a second, so it will not be able to measure the tiny amount of time light takes to travel 30 m *[1 mark]*.
b) Jacques would hear the gun after seeing it fire, as light travels faster than sound *[1 mark]*.
c) Light waves don't need particles to travel, but sound waves do *[1 mark]*. There aren't any particles in a vacuum so sound waves can't travel through it, but light can *[1 mark]*.

Page 98: Reflection

1   a) i) A line that is at right angles to the surface *[1 mark]*.
ii) The angle of incidence is equal to the angle of reflection *[1 mark]*.

b)

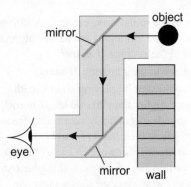

[1 mark for straight lines with correct arrows from object to eye and 1 mark for angle of incidence and reflection equal at each mirror]

2 a) Light rays from the sun are (diffusely) reflected/scattered off the prairie dog *[1 mark]*. Some of the reflected light enters the falcon's eyes *[1 mark]*.

b) It is not able to see the falcon. Since angle of incidence = angle of reflection *[1 mark]*, the light rays from the falcon are reflected to the opposite side of the pond to the prairie dog *[1 mark]*.

Page 99: Refraction

1 a) When the light passes from the water to the air at an angle to the normal it changes **direction**. This is known as **refraction**. *[1 mark]*

b) 0° *[1 mark]*

2 How to grade your answer:

0 marks:	There is no relevant information.
1-2 marks:	Some valid points are made, but the method is not described properly. The points made are not linked together.
3-4 marks:	The method is generally described well. Most of the main points are included. Some of the points made are linked together.
5-6 marks:	The method is described well, and covers all the main points and at least one of the extra points. The points made are well-linked and the answer has a clear and logical structure.

Here are some points your answer may include:

Main points
Draw the normal on the paper at the point where the ray enters the block, using a protractor and a ruler.
Use the markings on the paper to measure the angle of incidence and the angle of refraction of the ray as it enters the block using a protractor.
Repeat the experiment for a range of angles of incidence and measure the angle of refraction.
Repeat the measurement of the angle of refraction three or more times for each angle of incidence and take an average.

Extra points
Use a range of angles of incidence between, e.g., 20° and 80°.
Use a sharp pencil to draw the outline and the rays to avoid errors in measurements.

Pages 100-101: Transmission and Absorption of Light

1 a) dispersion *[1 mark]*

b) red *[1 mark]*

c) White light is made up of different colours *[1 mark]*. Different colours have different frequencies *[1 mark]*. Different frequencies are refracted by different amounts *[1 mark]*.

d) So that the light can be transmitted through the prism / so that the light is not absorbed or reflected by the prism *[1 mark]*.

e) E.g. In a rainbow *[1 mark]*, different colours are refracted by different amounts in raindrops *[1 mark]*.

2 a) i) The object absorbs the light then re-emits it in all directions *[1 mark]*.

ii) (diffuse) scattering *[1 mark]*

iii) tissue paper *[1 mark]*

b) transmitted *[1 mark]*

c) i) The light is transmitted through the object *[1 mark]*

ii) E.g. glass / water / diamond *[1 mark]*

3 a) colour/frequency of the light *[1 mark]*

b) angle of refraction / angle to the normal of the light travelling through the block *[1 mark]*

c) E.g. the glass block / angle of incidence/the incident angle of light on the block / light intensity / light beam width *[1 mark]*

Section P4 — Electricity and Electromagnetism

Page 102: Electrical Circuits

1 a) Flow of charge around a circuit *[1 mark]*.

b) Chemical energy from the battery is transformed into electrical energy, which flows round the circuit *[1 mark]*. The electrical energy is transferred to the bulb and is transformed into light energy *[1 mark]*.

c) Insulating material has a very high resistance. This will slow down the flow of current *[1 mark]*, so the bulb will not light *[1 mark]*.

d) i) It increases *[1 mark]*.

ii) It decreases *[1 mark]*.

iii) The current passing through each bulb isn't used up, so the current passing through them both is the same, so they shine equally brightly *[1 mark]*.

Pages 103-104: More on Electrical Circuits

1 an SPST *[1 mark]*

2

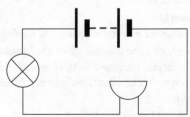

[1 mark for correctly drawing the battery, 1 mark for correctly drawing the bulb and 1 mark for correctly drawing the buzzer.]

3 a) The current supplied by the battery will decrease over time *[1 mark]*.

b) E.g. measure and record the current displayed on the ammeter at regular time intervals, e.g. every 30 minutes *[1 mark]*. Plot the results on a graph of current against time and draw a line of best fit *[1 mark]*.

4 a) A light emitting diode / LED *[1 mark]*

b) i) Ampere / Amp *[1 mark]*

ii) By using an ammeter *[1 mark]* placed in series with the component/circuit *[1 mark]*.

c) A fuse *[1 mark]*

5 a)

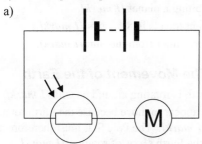

[1 mark for correctly drawing a motor and 1 mark for correctly drawing a light dependent resistor.]

b) The intensity of light shone on the light dependent resistor *[1 mark]*.

Pages 105-106: Series and Parallel Circuits

1 a) Bulbs 2 and 3 *[1 mark]*

b) Bulb 1 *[1 mark]*

2 a) They are in series because the current has no choice but to pass through them both *[1 mark]*.

b) There is no current/0 C passing through A_2. The branch of the circuit containing A_2 is broken by the open switch, so no current can pass through *[1 mark]*.

3

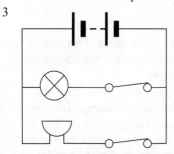

[1 mark for correctly drawing the bulb and buzzer, 1 mark for correctly drawing the battery, 1 mark for drawing the bulb and buzzer in parallel with one another and 1 mark for drawing switches on each branch of the circuit.]

4 a)

Ammeter	A_1	A_2	A_3	A_4	A_5
Reading (A)	9.2	3.9	2.6	2.7	9.2

[1 mark for each correct answer.]
The current at A_5 is equal to the current at A_1. The current of A_2, A_3 and A_4 must all add up to the current at A_1, so:
$A_4 = A_1 - A_2 - A_3 = 9.2 - 3.9 - 2.6 = 2.7 A$

b) Because if one light goes out and breaks the circuit, the other lights will still work *[1 mark]*.

Page 107: AND and OR Circuits

1 It is an AND circuit because current only flows through the bulb when both switch 1 and switch 2 are closed *[1 mark]*.

2

Input		Output
Switch A	Switch B	Bulb
F	F	F
T	F	T
F	T	T
T	T	T

[1 mark for each correct row.]

Pages 108-109: Magnets

1 a) A region where magnetic materials experience a force *[1 mark]*.

b)

[1 mark for correctly drawn field lines and 1 mark for field line arrows pointing from the North pole to the South pole.]

c) The needle of a compass is a small bar magnet *[1 mark]*. The Earth has a magnetic field which the needle of a compass aligns with, causing it to point North *[1 mark]*.

2 a) Only one of the blocks is a magnet *[1 mark]*.
If they were both magnets, they would repel each other in one of the two positions shown.

b) By holding each block next to a known magnet in different orientations *[1 mark]*. If a block is repulsed, it is a magnet *[1 mark]*.

3 a) E.g. the paperclip / the incline of the surface / the type of surface / the distance she starts from / the person doing the experiment *[1 mark]*.

b) E.g. by repeating the experiment multiple times / by measuring the distance at which the paperclip moves towards the magnet rather than using her judgement *[1 mark]*.

c)

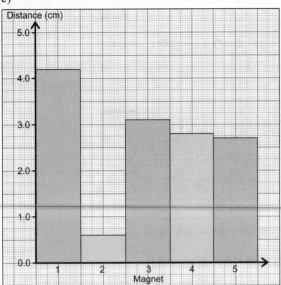

[1 mark for drawing a bar chart, 1 mark for using a sensible scale, 1 mark for correctly labelled axes, 1 mark for drawing bars accurately.]

Page 110: Electromagnets

1   a)   Wrap the wire in a coil around the iron bar *[1 mark]* and connect the ends of the wire to a power supply so that current is running through the wire *[1 mark]*.

    b)   Bar magnets always have a magnetic field (you can't turn it off), electromagnets can have their magnetic field turned off *[1 mark]*.

    c)   E.g. supply more current to the wire *[1 mark]* and add more turns to the coil *[1 mark]*.

    d)   Scatter the iron filings around the magnet and they will align along the magnetic field lines of the magnet *[1 mark]*.

2   a)   When the input circuit is switched on, the electromagnet's field is turned on *[1 mark]*. This causes the iron lever to be attracted to it, causing it to rotate *[1 mark]*. As it rotates the other end of the lever pushes the contacts together, which turns on the output circuit *[1 mark]*.

    b)   E.g. in lifting magnets / in direct current (DC) motors *[1 mark]*

Section P5 — Space Physics

Page 111: Gravity

1   There is always a gravitational force of **attraction** *[1 mark]* between two **masses** *[1 mark]*. This means that an object near the Earth's surface will fall towards the **Earth's centre** *[1 mark]*.

2   a)   The gravitational attraction between the mass of the Earth and the disc / the Earth's gravitational pull *[1 mark]*.

    b)   mass = weight ÷ gravitational field strength
        gravitational field strength on Earth = 10 N/kg
        weight of disc = 4 N
        so mass = 4 ÷ 10 = 0.4 kg
        [3 marks for the correct answer, otherwise 1 mark for using correct value of Earth's gravitational field strength and 1 mark for reading correct weight from the newton meter.]

    c)   weight = mass × gravitational field strength
        = 0.4 × 3.7 = 1.48 N
        [2 marks for correct answer, otherwise 1 mark for using answer to b) as the mass.]

Page 112: The Solar System and Beyond

1   a)   i)   Mercury *[1 mark]*
        ii)   the Milky Way *[1 mark]*

    b)   The gravitational force *[1 mark]* between the Sun and the planets *[1 mark]*.

    c)   Mars is further from the Sun *[1 mark]*.

    d)   E.g. a moon orbiting a planet *[1 mark]*.

2   a)   The distance light travels in 8.6 years *[1 mark]*.

    b)   The planets reflect light from the Sun *[1 mark]*.

Pages 113-114: The Movement of the Earth

1   a)   Because the Earth is rotating around its axis *[1 mark]*.

    b)   The other stars appear to move because the Earth rotates about its axis *[1 mark]*. The Pole Star must therefore be directly above the Earth's axis of rotation *[1 mark]*.

2   a)   When the Moon passes between the Sun and the Earth *[1 mark]*, blocking the light from the Sun from reaching the Earth *[1 mark]*.

    b)   i)

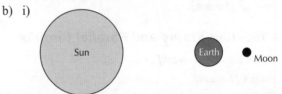

    [1 mark for drawing the Sun to the left of the Earth]

        ii)   The Moon is seen from sunlight reflected off its surface *[1 mark]*. The Earth blocks this light during an eclipse, so the Moon is less bright when viewed from Earth *[1 mark]*.

3   a)   i)   Japan *[1 mark]*
        ii)   The Earth completes half a rotation about its axis over 12 hours *[1 mark]*. So Japan will now be facing towards the Sun *[1 mark]*.

    b)   New York is tilted towards the Sun and Argentina is tilted away from the Sun in June *[1 mark]*. This means New York has longer days than Argentina, so New York has more hours of sunshine and more time to heat up *[1 mark]*. The Sun's rays are spread over a smaller area in the northern hemisphere than the southern hemisphere in June, so the heat is more focused in New York than in Argentina *[1 mark]*.

    c)   The Sun reaches a higher point in the sky in summer than in winter *[1 mark]*.

Page 115: Satellites

1   The Moon **is a satellite of the Earth** *[1 mark]*.

2   Any two from: e.g. in communication to relay radio/TV/telephone signals around the world / in navigation such as in satnavs and global positioning systems / to observe the Earth/satellite imaging / to monitor the weather / to explore the solar system *[2 marks — 1 mark for each correct answer]*.

3   a)   E.g. it's cheaper and safer than sending astronauts into space *[1 mark]*.

    b)   E.g. what conditions are like on Mars *[1 mark]*.